MURMURING JUDGES

JUDGES

DAVID HARE

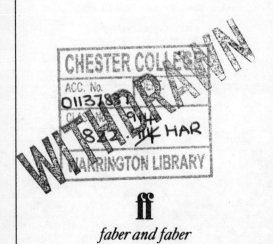
ff

faber and faber

LONDON · BOSTON

First published in 1991
by Faber and Faber Limited
3 Queen Square London WC1N 3AU

Photoset by Parker Typesetting Service, Leicester
Printed by Clays Ltd, St Ives plc

A CIP record for this book
is available from the British Library

ISBN 0-571-16587-7

For Richard

Murmuring Judges was first performed at the Olivier Theatre, London, on 10 October 1991. The cast was as follows:

Constabulary

PC SANDRA BINGHAM	Lesley Sharp
PS LESTER SPEED	Paul Moriarty
PC DAVE LAWRENCE	Keith Bartlett
PC TOBY METCALFE	Simon Coates
PC ESTHER BALLY	Sally Rogers
DC BARRY HOPPER	Keith Allen
DC ABDUL 'JIMMY' KHAN	Paul Bhattacharjee

Bench and Bar

JUDGE	Jeffrey Segal
MR JUSTICE CUDDEFORD	Michael Bryant
SIR PETER EDGECOMBE QC	Richard Pasco
IRINA PLATT	Alphonsia Emmanuel
WOODY PEARSON	Tim McMullan
TOASTMASTER	Doyne Byrd

Prison Service

PO RAYMOND BECKETT	Joseph O'Connor

Government

RT HON. KEVIN CUMBERLAND MP	Peter Wight

Clients

GERARD MCKINNON	Robert Patterson
KEITH MACHIN	Paul Wyett
WOMAN UNDER ARREST	Judith Coke
FRIEND	Judy Damas
BANGLADESHI MAN	Royce Hounsell
BANGLADESHI WOMAN	Sandra James-Young
JASON SMITH	Tyrone Huggins
'NELSON'	Walter Hall
FIRST PRISONER	Andrew Woodall
SECOND PRISONER	John Adewole

Police, barristers, court officers, prisoners, etc.

Director	Richard Eyre
Designer	Bob Crowley
Lighting	Mark Henderson
Music	Richard Hartley

ACT ONE

ACT TWO

AUTHOR'S NOTE

I was helped in the writing of this play by the special kindness and patience of many people from the police force, the bar, the bench and the prison service. I welcome this chance to thank them all. Faults of understanding are mine alone.

Murmuring Judges is the second play in an intended trilogy about British institutions. The first play, *Racing Demon*, was about the Church of England. The title of this play is from a legal expression, meaning to speak ill of the judiciary. It is still an offence in Scottish law.

So long as a judge keeps silent,
his reputation for wisdom and impartiality remains unassailable.
Lord Chancellor Kilmuir

Professional people have no cares
Whatever happens they get theirs
Ogden Nash

ACT ONE

SCENE ONE

An empty stage. Then suddenly from nowhere, they're all there – the judge, the jury, the battery of lawyers in wigs, the public, the police, the press, the ushers, the guards and, at the centre of the forward-facing court, the defendants. The entire company of the law has appeared in the blinking of an eye.

At the centre, the three defendants, of whom GERARD MCKINNON *is conspicuously the youngest, barely in his twenties, thin, wiry, tall, his dark hair down to his shoulders. Beside him, crop-haired, pale, in suits, two other defendants,* TRAVIS *and* FAULKNER. *But the emphasis of the light is on* MCKINNON, *and before you're ready he begins to speak. He has an Irish accent.*

GERARD: I'm standing here, I'm thinking, oh God, it's coming, it *is* coming, it's finally happening, hold on, remember this is happening to me. After it going so slowly, *slowly*, the standing, the waiting – God, is there anything in the world slower than a lawyer? – after all that, now suddenly, hold on, stop, *stop*, hold on, suddenly it's going so fast . . .
(*The lights change to favour the whole court as the* USHER *calls to make everyone stand.*)
USHER: Will the court please rise?
CLERK: Have you considered your verdict?
JURYMAN: We have.
CLERK: Do you find the defendants guilty or not guilty?
(*A slight pause.*)
JURYMAN: Guilty.
(*The lights change again as* GERARD *struggles to interrupt.*)
GERARD: And I want to say, yes, hold on, just a moment, fair enough, take me back, I did meet these men, yes, I did, but I thought at the time, part of me thought, this is stupid; I mean, be fair, I know this is meant to be real, but I'm not *really* doing this, there's a part of me which isn't standing here on this freezing pavement, thinking how did I get myself into this? So why is it now, only now, yes, *now*, just at this moment, why is everything finally real?

I

(*The lights change back to favour the court.*)

JUDGE: And now I will turn to the sentencing. Please, will the prisoners attend?

(*The lights focus on* GERARD, *his speech now more insistent than ever.*)

GERARD: Finally I get it, yes, it *is* happening, these men, every one of them silver-haired, judicious, informed, they will go home to their wives, to wine in fine glasses and the gossip of the Bar, they will walk the streets and laugh and complain about their lives, and I . . . (*He stops; more insistently*) And *I* . . .

(*The court is lit again.*)

JUDGE: For Travis, eight years and six years to run concurrently. For Faulkner, eight years and six concurrently also. For McKinnon . . . (*A pause.*) Five years.

(*The lights change, as if* GERARD *were at last alone. He is quiet.*)

GERARD: And *I* . . . the stuff of their profession . . . I will go to my gaol.

SCENE TWO

The court at once melds into the incoming scene, led by the defence counsel, who walk from the court towards us. At the centre of the action is SIR PETER EDGECOMBE QC, *who is tall, thin, fastidious, in his early sixties, with a slightly raffish appearance which contradicts the precision of his speech.*

The new scene is in a corridor area which gives on to the High Court. Stretching away far into the distance is the Hall of the Court, a great vaulted Victorian building, which is marked for us by the small knots of people standing around. It is ten to two, and the courts are about to resume; a massive perspective is given to the area by the groups of lawyers and clients who are consulting just before the courts resume.

At the very front, MR JUSTICE CUDDEFORD *is coming along a corridor on his way to work. He is in his early sixties, a large, bald man, heavily built, incisive. As soon as he sees* SIR PETER *he greets him ironically.*

CUDDEFORD: Sir Peter!

SIR PETER: Judge!

    (*They smile contentedly.*)

CUDDEFORD: Are you looking crestfallen?

SIR PETER: Crestfallen? Am I? No, I don't think so.

CUDDEFORD: They were saying at lunch you'd just lost your case.

SIR PETER: Good Lord, I'm astonished anyone mentioned it.

CUDDEFORD: But they did.

SIR PETER: It was a very trivial affair. (*He smiles, unruffled.*) I'm
    already on to my next one.

CUDDEFORD: Naturally.

SIR PETER: That's why I'm here. I only took the criminal case as
    a favour. Fair dos, Desmond. I came to it late.

CUDDEFORD: They all count. It spoils your bowling average.

SIR PETER: Hardly. Beaky Harris was meant to be leading the
    defence.

    (CUDDEFORD *smiles, as if we all know* BEAKY.)

    But his horse was running in Paris. And I owed him one. It
    turned out to be a silly sort of warehouse robbery. And
    Beaky didn't leave me much of a case.

    (*He smiles.* IRINA PLATT *is standing one dutiful pace behind her
    silk. She is black, in her mid-twenties, neat, well-presented,
    open-faced, with a quiet politeness which is hard to interpret.*)

CUDDEFORD: I was hoping to run into you. Because I heard you
    yesterday.

SIR PETER: Yesterday?

CUDDEFORD: I don't mean in court.

SIR PETER: Oh, I see. (*He smoothly introduces* IRINA.) You
    haven't met our new tenant?

CUDDEFORD: No.

SIR PETER: She's just joined our chambers. She was a
    Commonwealth scholar. Irina Platt. Mr Justice Cuddeford.

CUDDEFORD: Excellent.

IRINA: How do you do?

    (CUDDEFORD *smiles slyly at* SIR PETER.)

CUDDEFORD: We were just discussing Sir Peter's latest public
    manifestation.

IRINA: Oh, yes.

CUDDEFORD: You heard it?

IRINA: I did.

SIR PETER: I do sometimes think it's the last remaining thing the British all hold in common. It's the only time we're really one nation.

CUDDEFORD: It's true.

SIR PETER: Just for that moment, with all our differences, all our different attitudes to life, nevertheless before Sunday lunchtime, the whole nation stops and comes together.

CUDDEFORD: Yes, yes, I agree.

(SIR PETER *smiles modestly*.)

SIR PETER: It's extraordinary. Everyone listens to *Desert Island Discs*.

(IRINA *looks down, impassive*.)

CUDDEFORD: I liked the Brahms.

SIR PETER: Yes, I was saying to Irina at the Bailey this morning, I accepted to do it not in any way for myself . . .

CUDDEFORD: No.

SIR PETER: I had no personal motive at all. It's pure chance I've featured in a few eye-catching cases . . .

CUDDEFORD: Indeed.

SIR PETER: So for that reason my name is known. I wanted to speak on the programme on behalf of the whole profession at large.

(CUDDEFORD *looks at him a moment*.)

CUDDEFORD: I see.

SIR PETER: Not least at this moment. People have such forbidding ideas of our character. It seems to me not bad to show there is another side. (*He smiles*.) More human, perhaps. More fallible, even.

CUDDEFORD: Yes. (*He frowns thoughtfully*.) I'm not sure your records quite reflected that aim.

SIR PETER: What do you mean?

CUDDEFORD: Edith Piaf. If 'fallible' is how you wished to appear . . . it's none of my business . . .

SIR PETER: Please . . .

CUDDEFORD: Maybe '*Non, je ne regrette rien*' didn't quite hit the mark.

(SIR PETER *turns to* IRINA, *about to defend himself, but* CUDDEFORD *rides over him*.)

4

SIR PETER: Well . . .

CUDDEFORD: I admit it came out of a discussion of your private life.

SIR PETER: Yes. I couldn't stop that.

CUDDEFORD: Why should you? It was informative. A whistle-stop tour of your wives. It was nice to catch up, so to speak. But I admit to one ugly moment. I thought, oh my goodness, he's out of control. But I misjudged you. You spared us 'My Way'.

(SIR PETER *is a little discomfited by this in front of* IRINA.)

SIR PETER: The Piaf meant nothing, Desmond. I just like her voice.

(CUDDEFORD *looks confidently at* IRINA, *enjoying himself*.)

CUDDEFORD: Miss Platt, please ignore these old battles between us. It's probably jealousy. Peter and I started at the same time.

IRINA: Yes.

CUDDEFORD: But he chose one path. Star advocate.

SIR PETER: Desmond went the other way.

CUDDEFORD: That's right. It's my nature to sit in judgment. To be above the battle. To allow all points of view.

(*They are both smiling now*.)

SIR PETER: We regard Irina as a catch.

CUDDEFORD: I see that.

SIR PETER: She seemed to us to have all the assets we need in a forward-looking bar.

CUDDEFORD: Yes. I see those. Most clearly.

SIR PETER: She was the unanimous choice. Of the whole of chambers. We all felt she is exactly the very kind of person the Bar is now most eager to attract.

CUDDEFORD: Yes.

(*He smiles at* IRINA *who has been quite still through all this, looking down*.)

SIR PETER: Mind you, the first day we had a bit of a problem. May I tell this story?

IRINA: Yes.

SIR PETER: Irina turned up to court in a rather brilliant green dress.

CUDDEFORD: Green? Oh, my goodness.

(*Both men smile, a shared pleasure in this.*)

I suppose everyone told you what old Chugger used to do?

IRINA: No.

SIR PETER: Chugger was a famous old judge.

CUDDEFORD: He'd say to a lady barrister, 'I'm sorry, I can't hear you.' She'd start speaking louder. 'I still can't hear you.' She'd say, 'Do you have a problem with my diction, my Lord?' 'No, I don't think so,' he'd say. 'I just sense I'd hear you more clearly if you attended the court wearing black.' (*He wheezes with laughter.*) Outrageous!

SIR PETER: Yes.

CUDDEFORD: Absolutely outrageous.

(IRINA *frowns slightly.*)

IRINA: But they still don't like it.

CUDDEFORD: Well, no.

IRINA: Sir Peter suggested I change.

CUDDEFORD: Yes. There is a serious point, I'm afraid. It's the judge's court. It's his. He runs it as he sees fit. And, in English law, it's very important he does.

(CUDDEFORD *is pleased with this, but* IRINA *is impassive, her own view hidden.*)

SIR PETER: Irina has been doing her bit for all our freedoms.

CUDDEFORD: Oh, really?

SIR PETER: Yes. I've sent her out collecting for our Bar Council fund.

CUDDEFORD: I heard rumour of a fund.

SIR PETER: We've decided to employ a well-known firm of public-relations consultants.

CUDDEFORD: Well, good.

SIR PETER: People need to understand just what a threat to justice the new legislation might be.

CUDDEFORD: Indeed.

SIR PETER: If we were to merge the functions of barrister and solicitor, if any move were made to dismantle the specialist Bar, I don't think the public begin to appreciate just how disastrous the consequences would be.

(CUDDEFORD *looks at him a moment.*)

CUDDEFORD: No.

SIR PETER: We started fund-raising for a campaign about four days ago.

CUDDEFORD: How much have you raised?

IRINA: One million.

> (CUDDEFORD *turns and looks at her a moment. There is a sudden silence.*)

CUDDEFORD: That sounds an auspicious start. One million?

SIR PETER: As you say.

IRINA: Give or take a few thousand.

CUDDEFORD: Well, well.

> (IRINA'*s gaze does not waver from* CUDDEFORD. *He is thoughtful.* SIR PETER *smiles, breaking the mood.*)

SIR PETER: It's been an education, of course, for Irina.

CUDDEFORD: I'm sure.

SIR PETER: It means she's met nearly every leading member of our profession. In chambers, I mean.

CUDDEFORD: Yes.

IRINA: I wouldn't claim to have met them. They've given me a cheque. (*She smiles.*) I've been given a cheque by some of the most respected barristers alive.

CUDDEFORD: Has anyone refused?

IRINA: No. No one.

CUDDEFORD: Remarkable.

SIR PETER: Yes. I think it underlines the profound depth of feeling. What did the Lord Chief say? 'Tyranny does not always arrive with a toothbrush moustache and wearing a swastika'?

CUDDEFORD: He did say that.

SIR PETER: Yes. (SIR PETER *turns, at ease again now, on familiar ground.*) Of course it seems strange. It will take getting used to. For years the bar has simply been there. We have existed. Without any need to justify ourselves. And now suddenly, bingo! No longer taken for granted. We are no longer exempt. We must take our case to the marketplace, not just for ourselves, but on behalf of everyone who values professional life. (*He smiles in anticipation of his next, mischievous thought.*) And when some . . . shady Tory politician discovers he's accused of accidentally overspending his election fund, then obviously at that moment, when he reaches for the phone and says, 'Get me an expert, get me the finest specialist forensic advocate in the land,' then at that point . . . when he needs us . . . then he will know the folly of diluting our profession. He will feel it, oh yes, most urgently. As urgently as if there were no electric light. (*He looks to them, his performance suspended before its coda.*) But until then, Desmond, the duty falls to us, I would say, to protect these politicians from their own worst instincts. (*He nods to himself.*) And I don't know anyone who doesn't see it that way.

(CUDDEFORD *smiles, quietly amused by this speech.*)

CUDDEFORD: You will work with this man?

IRINA: Yes.

CUDDEFORD: You are fortunate. You impress me, Peter. As always. *Quod erat demonstrandum.* Your case is proved. (*He pauses a second, watchful.*) I would enter only one caveat perhaps.

SIR PETER: What's that?

CUDDEFORD: The sum of money which Miss Platt has collected. (*He leans in a moment.*) Keep that to yourself. Why don't you? (*He smiles.*) *Verb sap.* If the whole world is now to be public relations. Play down the million, Sir Peter.

(*Immediately beside him the* CLERK *of his court has appeared, gowned and respectful. The Hall behind has emptied and there is a sudden hush now.*)

CLERK: Sir, the court is ready for you.

CUDDEFORD: Good. (*He turns to them.*) I must go and do some judging.

SIR PETER *and* IRINA: (*Together*) Judge.

(*There is a slight formality now, and* IRINA *even bows slightly.*)

CUDDEFORD: I trust I'll see you again.

(*He turns and goes.* IRINA *and* SIR PETER *stand a moment, etched in the light from the high windows. Then they part, going separate ways, and the stage lightens.*)

SCENE THREE

IRINA *turns from the courts, leaving* SIR PETER *to go on in, and with her papers tucked under her arm sets off towards the Inns of Court. It's a fine sunny day, and she strides confidently across. As she does, she is joined by* WOODY PEARSON, *who is in his thirties, pencil-thin, clever, in a grey suit. He has a cockney accent. They head together towards Sir Peter's chambers.*

WOODY: Miss Platt, there you are.

IRINA: Good afternoon, Woody.

WOODY: I hear that one turned out to be a pile of piss.

(*She hands him back the brief.*)

IRINA: It wasn't a great case.

WOODY: Yeah. I thought Beaky made a pretty smart move.

IRINA: Was it deliberate?

WOODY: Well, he has this sort of allergy, you know. When he hears the words 'legal aid'.

IRINA: Oh, I see. His horse wasn't running?

WOODY: What do I know?

(*They have arrived at the chambers and gone into the outer office. WOODY starts sorting out briefs, which he hands to her.*)

This has just come in. You're in Kingston in the morning. Defending an a.b.h. All right? Then I hope we're going to get you over to Southwark. It's just for an adjournment. Have you got a car?

IRINA: Sure.

WOODY: How fast is it? Can you squeeze in a quick plea in Brighton? It shouldn't take long. You can read it while you're driving.

(*IRINA smiles at him ironically.*)

No? Really? Go your own pace. (*He takes the third brief back.*)

IRINA: What about that interim injunction? Sir Peter wants me as his junior on that.

WOODY: Oh yeah, that's Thursday. But Sir Peter says he wants you both to work on it tonight.

IRINA: Sir Peter says?

WOODY: Yeah.

IRINA: (*Frowns*) I was just with him at the High Court.

WOODY: You're to go and take in a little Mozart, he said. Then you'll work on here afterwards.

(*IRINA stops a moment, frowning.*)

IRINA: Woody, he could have just said.

WOODY: But he doesn't need to, does he? That's what he asks me for.

9

IRINA: I think there's a word for what he's asking you to do.

WOODY: I know that word. 'Clerking.'

IRINA: Is that what it's called?

(*They both smile. It's easy-going between them, but* WOODY *is behaving as if this is all quite usual.*)

WOODY: It's all right, don't fret, it's just for appearances. It's nothing more. He goes to Covent Garden, he wants something nice to hold his right arm. To be *seen* to hold his right arm. (*He throws a quick glance at her.*) Ease up. It happens.

IRINA: Since you're the intermediary, tell him the answer is no.

(WOODY *is not thrown for a second.*)

WOODY: No? OK, I'll write that down, so I don't get it wrong. Just remind me: opera, invitation, message from the new girl, sorry, afraid she won't go.

IRINA: I didn't say sorry.

WOODY: No. I invented that. It must have been the last one.

IRINA: What do you mean?

WOODY: The last new girl we had here. Very bright. From Harvard. I was told she was an absolute whiz with her torts. She said no. As I recall, to Wagner. Well, fair enough. I avoid anything where people sing in helmets.

(*He looks at* IRINA; *then softly*) But look at it the other way. Where is she now? (*He looks at her a moment.*) Come on, it's fine. Just think for a moment. Imagine you were a bloke. There wouldn't be a problem.

IRINA: If I were a man, he wouldn't ask me.

WOODY: Look, this is how business is done. The world over. (*He smiles.*) If you work in the law, there's a lot of big issues. A lot of big questions come along. It's quite plain, you're pretty feisty, the time is going to come when you want to make a stand. About something, I don't know what. (*He pauses, suddenly quiet and serious for the first time.*) Don't waste it on something which really doesn't matter. Like whether you're in the Crush Bar tonight. Why put his back up? Why start badly? It's innocent. He's a decent man. He's flash but he's decent. It's good advice. Fight when it matters. Because, surely to God, that moment will come.

(IRINA *is watching him closely, hearing all this. But then she shakes her head.*)

IRINA: I'm saying no. It's beginning wrong. It's the wrong start.
(WOODY *thinks a moment, looking down, still gentle.*)
WOODY: You see, the thing is, Irina, the point is, it's a team.
There's a lot of latitude. But you play in a team. You want to
start inside, not outside.
IRINA: I know that. (*She smiles at him, touched by his genuine
concern.*) Thank you, Woody. (*She turns and goes into her
office.*) And now I'm going to get some work done.

SCENE FOUR

*The stage darkens and we move into the enormous gloomy space of the
prison reception area. The prison is Victorian, with a gigantic door just
discernible at the back. It is late night, with only a few high lights
making shapes through the gloom. What by day is a busy area, with a
very long desk running along one side, is now deserted and quiet.*
RAYMOND BECKETT, *in his fifties, large, balding, with a big stomach
beneath his blue pullover, is sitting waiting behind the desk. He has a
open, blunt manner.*
At once from the back GERARD *is escorted out of the darkness by a
short, foxy-looking* OFFICER *who brings him in to face* BECKETT.

BECKETT: Strip off.
GERARD: I'm sorry?
BECKETT: Empty all your pockets and take off your clothes.
(GERARD, *a little bewildered, looks round the huge space. The
other* OFFICER *has already disappeared into the darkness at the
other side of the area.*)
GERARD: Here?
(*Catching* GERARD's *tone,* BECKETT *looks up from the
admission sheets.*)
BECKETT: Don't you know the procedures? Haven't you been in
prison before?
GERARD: No.
BECKETT: Weren't you on remand?
GERARD: I was on bail.
BECKETT: Were you? So is this your first time?
(GERARD *looks at him, not needing to answer.*)

Why aren't you emptying your pockets?

(GERARD *moves to the desk and empties his pockets on to it.*
BECKETT *puts the stuff in a plastic bag.*)

Here. Your things will go in this bag.

(GERARD *starts to undress. The silent* OFFICER *has started to sort
through what looks like a pile of rags.*)

Why are you so late?

GERARD: They took me to Pentonville. But then it turned out
there wasn't any room.

BECKETT: There's no room here. But we'll make some. Why is it
midnight?

GERARD: Then there wasn't a van.

BECKETT: Again?

GERARD: They couldn't find one.

BECKETT: Have you eaten?

GERARD: I had some spaghetti. But then I lost it.

BECKETT: How are you feeling?

GERARD: Not very well.

(BECKETT *is filling in forms. The other* OFFICER, *non-
committal, now goes to lean against the desk a long way off. He
lights a cigarette, says nothing, just watches.*)

BECKETT: We've put you on D-wing. We shouldn't really. It's for
lifers. But it's that or sleeping in the chapel.

(*There is a sudden silence.* GERARD *is in the middle of the area,
covering his nakedness with his hand. His clothes are in a pile
beside him.* BECKETT *holds out the form on a clipboard to the
naked man.*)

Sign here.

GERARD: I can't. You've taken my pen.

(BECKETT *looks at him a moment, as if not sure whether the
mildness of* GERARD's *manner is a subtle form of piss-take.*
GERARD *signs.*)

BECKETT: Would you like a cigarette?

GERARD: No, thank you.

BECKETT: You're meant to have a shower. But the water's off. So
you can get dressed.

GERARD: I'm sorry?

BECKETT: There's a pile of clothes over there.

(*He points towards the heap.* GERARD *goes over and starts pulling clothes out of it.*)

Gerard McKinnon.

GERARD: Yes.

BECKETT: I'm giving you a number. All right? A6324. That's what you'll answer to. Do you need to hear it again?

GERARD: No, I've got it.

BECKETT: The governor will come and see you in the morning. And we'll fix you with a job. You're going to have to work. Prison isn't just sitting around.

GERARD: No. (*He is frowning at the outsize tops and trousers, while at the same time trying to stay decent.*) No, I know that.

BECKETT: You'll see all the departments. There's a reception committee. Probation officer, medical, educational. The chaplain. They'll advise you on how to survive in the gaol.

GERARD: Survive?

BECKETT: Just so you don't waste your time. It's up to you. You can make this place work for you. Anyone can. It's not hard. Get educated. Be sensible.

GERARD: Yes. (*He stops a moment, hesitating to speak, halfway dressed.*) It's silly. You see, I was sent down with two other people. I was expecting they'd be here with me.

BECKETT: That's not the policy.

GERARD: No. I'm not complaining. I don't like them that much. It's just . . . they're more experienced. So I thought they might sort of see me through.

BECKETT: Yeah. (*He is looking hard at* GERARD.) Look, I think someone better tell you. Before you get started. You'd better learn. I've seen people go crazy if it's their first time. (*He pauses a moment.*) What you have to do is put the past behind you. Do you understand?

(GERARD *frowns a moment, as he dresses.*)

You got done. You did wrong. Society's put you in gaol. OK, now don't brood. Work to the future. Work to the moment when you get out.

GERARD: Yes, I see.

BECKETT: Because you know what's most dangerous?

GERARD: No, I don't.

BECKETT: The worst is getting bitter. That's the thing. I watch it. That's the thing that messes people up. Do you see? If you get an attitude. If you get an attitude, I tell you, it's worse than catching the clap. (*He suddenly raises his voice across the area, without warning.*) An attitude's the clap. Do you understand me?

GERARD: What sort of attitude?

BECKETT: If you start thinking, they done me wrong, I'm always in the right, I hate this place, I shouldn't be here, and, pardon my French, sod you all, if you think that, then it kills you. You're finished. It burns you up.

GERARD: Yes. (*He looks at him nervously.*) I'll tell you what worries me.

BECKETT: Yes?

GERARD: I got a wife.

BECKETT: OK.

GERARD: She's not my wife actually. But we have two little children. One of them has Down's.

BECKETT: Yes. Go on.

GERARD: Down's syndrome, you see. (*He pauses, emotion about to overwhelm him for a moment.*) And I'm not sure how they'll keep their heads above water.

(*He stands a moment, the clothes ridiculously big for him.*)

BECKETT: Right, well, that's it, that's what I'm saying. There's some people here going to help you with that. There's people with degrees from Oxford University. They're giving up their lives to help you adjust. So you can live with being banged up.

(*He gets up now, to go and pick up the old clothes* GERARD *has discarded on the floor, and to put them in a bag.*)

It's a long job. It's not always easy. It's not like changing your clothes.

(BECKETT *is now standing directly opposite* GERARD. *His original clothes are in a plastic bag, while* GERARD *is like Charlie Chaplin, his trousers puddling round his feet, his jacket swamping him.*)

GERARD: Do you have a belt?

BECKETT: You're not allowed a belt. You'll kill yourself. (*He nods a moment.*) Do you want a cup of tea?

GERARD: I won't, thank you.

(*There's a moment's pause, things oddly formal and polite.*)

I'd like to sleep.

BECKETT: Good. You look good.

GERARD: Thank you.

(BECKETT *looks to the other* OFFICER.)

BECKETT: Shall we go up?

SCENE FIVE

Before they have gone, PC SANDRA BINGHAM *has appeared. She is in uniform, in her mid-twenties, with neat, dyed-blond, short hair. She is quite small and tidy. She speaks directly to us. As she does so, the gaol is replaced by the charge room of a large South London police station. A long desk dominates the room, and opposite it is a self-locking door which gives on to the outside world. Beside that is a long bench for the public. To one side of the long room is a passage which leads to the cells; to the other, the front desk of the police station.*

We are aware of the activity in the room behind as SANDRA *speaks to us, but the emphasis of the light is on her.*

SANDRA: You see, it's all mess. That's what it is, mostly. If you take the charge room, for instance, there's maybe thirty or forty people arrested in a day. Most of them are people who simply can't cope. They've been arrested before – petty thieving, deception, stealing car radios, selling stolen credit cards in pubs. Or not even that. Disturbing the peace. Failing to appear on a summons. Failing to carry out conditions of bail. Failing to produce a current car licence. Failing to fulfil community service. Getting drunk. Getting drunk and going for a joyride. Getting drunk and then driving home. Attacking your wife. Who then won't testify. Trying to cash a stolen cheque, only being so stupid you don't even try to make the signatures match. Opening telephone boxes. Fifty–fifty fights in clubs which are nobody's fault. Crimes of opportunity. Not being able to resist it. Then going back, thinking I got away with it last time. Possession. One acid tab. One Ninja Turtle sticker containing LSD. One smoke. One sniff. One toke. One three-quid packet. (*She smiles.*)

That's the basic stuff. It's the stuff of policing. All you have to do with it is be a ledger clerk. You fill in bits of paper. Every officer carries thirty-six bits of paper about their person at any one time.

(SANDRA *starts to move round the room to collect the boy she has just arrested. She stops a moment, before the scene begins.*)

Policing's largely the fine art of getting through biros. And keeping yourself ready for the interesting times.

(*At once the lights change and the scene begins with* SANDRA *coming through the door which leads to the outside world with* KEITH, *an obstreperous seventeen-year-old boy, who is in an extremely touchy and aggressive mood. He is surprisingly slight for someone who looks ready to pick a fight with anyone. At the desk* SERGEANT LESTER SPEED *is sitting, filling out forms. He is in his late thirties, with a loud voice; powerful, heavily built. He effortlessly dominates the room. Sitting on a desk behind him is* ESTHER BALLY, *a smart, young, dark-haired policewoman, who is busy on the phone.*)

KEITH: I didn't bloody do it. Don't bloody touch me.

SANDRA: What is this?

(*She lets* KEITH *go, affronted by his behaviour. The boy makes several feints, lifting his arms as if to protect himself from being handled again.*)

KEITH: Leave me. Just leave me.

SANDRA: I'm not touching you.

KEITH: Leave me.

SANDRA: I'm not touching you, all right?

(KEITH *moves away, standing right up against the wall, cowering, twenty feet from* SANDRA. LESTER *just watches.*)

KEITH: Don't bloody touch me.

SANDRA: I'm not bloody touching you.

LESTER: Good morning, Sandra.

SANDRA: Nice to see you, Sergeant.

(*She turns to* KEITH. *There is a moment's stalemate.*)

This is your custody officer. It's his job to tell you your rights.

(LESTER *reaches down to get out the appropriate form from his desk.*)

LESTER: I need a 57.

KEITH: I'm not saying anything.

LESTER: Sit down.

KEITH: I'm not sitting down.

LESTER: You'll have to sit eventually.

KEITH: You're a bloody pig.

LESTER: It's true. You're very observant. (*He has started filling in the form.*) God, have you had this all the way here?

SANDRA: Yes, I have, Sarge.

LESTER: You should be chuffed. Sandra's one of our high-flyers. It's very rare Sandra's not got her head in her books. Isn't that right?

SANDRA: Absolutely right.

(*He smiles to himself as he writes.*)

LESTER: She's in the fast lane. You should be flattered she's brought in a body at all. Let alone *you*.

(KEITH *looks at him mistrustfully.*)

KEITH: I'm not saying anything.

LESTER: Then don't.

KEITH: I don't want to be here.

LESTER: I don't want to be here either. I want to be in bed with Michelle Pfeiffer. But what we're talking about is what's called reality. Name?

(*Wordlessly,* KEITH *climbs on to the bench and stands on top of it, leaning against the wall.* LESTER *takes no notice.*)

Thank you, Sandra, now the rundown on the arrest.

(SANDRA *is opposite* LESTER, *also taking no notice of* KEITH.)

SANDRA: I was in Redwood Road, I saw this young man, leaning against a car, applying pressure to the handle. When he saw me, he started to run . . .

LESTER: OK . . .

SANDRA: I caught up, I got hold of him, I told him I was authorized to search his pockets . . . I found this.

(*She puts a small brown lump down on the desk.* LESTER *at once reaches down to another drawer in the desk to get a plastic bag and seal it.*)

And that's a small piece of what I think is dope.

KEITH: She bloody put it on me.

LESTER: Oh, you're talking.

KEITH: She put it in my pocket.

(LESTER *breaks off from writing, looks up, smiling slightly.*)

LESTER: I wouldn't say that, if I were you.

KEITH: Why the hell not?

LESTER: Because if you make an allegation against an officer, it's very serious, I have to fill in a completely different form. *And I've started this one.* (*He smiles.*) Do you get my point? Do you get what I mean?

(*At once through the door comes a fresh group: two women guided in by two thickly clad policemen. The older* WOMAN *is in her forties, in a pink velour jumpsuit; her* FRIEND, *in jeans, looks much younger.*)

Oh God, it looks like crime's back in fashion again.

(*The older of the two policemen is* DAVE LAWRENCE, *a jug-eared Welshman, stubby, in his fifties. He is putting the woman's handbag and purse down on the desk, while she is guided to the bench by* TOBY METCALFE, *an almost embarrassingly young, fair-haired Yorkshire boy.* SANDRA *meanwhile goes to sit down on the other side of the desk and write up her notes.*)

DAVE: I brought this couple in, Sarge. I was called along by Sainsbury's. It's on suspicion of chequebook fraud.

LESTER: All right, they'll have to wait, there's a queue.

WOMAN: I'm not sitting there.

(LESTER *waves airily at* KEITH, *who is still standing on the bench.*)

LESTER: Please, go and stand there next to him. It makes no difference to me.

WOMAN: I don't like the look of it.

DAVE: Esther, can you do a quick frisk?

(*The woman's* FRIEND *has begun to cry.*)

WOMAN: She's not feeling well.

LESTER: No, well, I'm not feeling wonderful.

(*The* FRIEND *is crying in the woman's arms.*)

DAVE: You all right, my love?

WOMAN: She had cancer, you see.

LESTER: Uh-huh.

(*He pauses a moment, uncharacteristically lost for words, then, to divert, turns to* TOBY.)

You all right?

TOBY: Me? Fine. (*He frowns.*) I'm fine, Sarge.

LESTER: So, who's going to do the report?

TOBY: Oh, well . . .

DAVE: You get some practice, Toby.

(DAVE *and* ESTHER *are attending to the* WOMEN, *while* TOBY *goes to the desk to make the formal report.*)

TOBY: Well, we were called in by the check-out manager at Sainsbury's. Look at these – you see, the signatures don't match. Here, their real names are on their family supplement books. And so . . . well, we made a joint decision, me and Dave.

LESTER: Astonishing. Unaided?

TOBY: We felt we had grounds for bringing them in.

(LESTER *nods and raises his voice.*)

LESTER: You're being detained. Do you understand what's happening?

WOMAN: Of course. I'm not stupid.

LESTER: Is she all right now?

WOMAN: She's OK.

LESTER: I'm reading you your rights. Do you want a solicitor?

(*The* WOMEN *look at one another uncertainly.*)

We'll get you the duty one.

ESTHER: What's happening with the frisking?

DAVE: Nothing. It's abandoned.

(DAVE *shakes his head.* LESTER *is holding out two forms for them.*)

LESTER: Sign. Your real name.

(*As the* WOMEN *move across to sign,* LESTER *turns to* ESTHER.)

Can you call that solicitor?

ESTHER: Sure.

LESTER: Abu ben Dhabi, or whatever he's called.

(*He keeps pointing to other places for the* WOMEN *to sign.*)

And here. He's of the Asian persuasion.

DAVE: Nothing wrong with that.

LESTER: 'Course you'd say that. Because you're a bloody Taffy.

DAVE: Yes, I am. And proud of it.

LESTER: And here. Oh yeah? All you bloody nationalists. If you're so proud of it, why d'you drive up the M4 every ten days? Go on, tell me.

DAVE: Because the money's better.

LESTER: OK. You're culturally dependent, mate. And don't you forget it.

DAVE: Don't think there's much chance of that.

(LESTER *takes back the forms*.)

LESTER: Thank you. Now, please – I'm sorry, this is all we have. This is our hospitality suite. You might as well use it. I think you're going to have a long wait.

(*Now from the front desk of the station in come two plainclothes men, both holding plastic cups.* BARRY HOPPER *is in his mid-thirties, cheerful, outgoing, wearing thick, dark glasses, like a film star. Beside him is* ABDUL KHAN, *known as* JIMMY, *spry, lightweight beside* BARRY *and a real snappy dresser, with shining black shoes.*)

BARRY: Good morning, all.

DAVE: Oh God, here they come. Wreathed in garlands.

(BARRY *makes a mock bow to the room*.)

BARRY: Just talented. Me and my partner. Just supremely talented. If you have any problems, please do call CID.

LESTER: I thought you'd be on a bloody chariot today.

BARRY: Take no notice, Jimmy.

JIMMY: I shan't.

BARRY: It's simple jealousy. Yes, we did manage rather a big case, since you ask.

JIMMY: Nothing to it.

(LESTER *looks admiringly at Jimmy's suit*.)

LESTER: I like the whistle, Jimmy.

JIMMY: Well, thank you.

LESTER: If I was a shit-hot detective, do you think they'd let me dress up like that?

JIMMY: I don't know, Lester. It's how you wear it that counts.

(DAVE *grins at this*.)

DAVE: Did you see the carpenters?

BARRY: What carpenters?

LESTER: You must have seen them. They're widening all the doors.

DAVE: Yeah. To get Barry's head through.

LESTER: Got a hangover, Barry? The glasses are good.

BARRY: My eyes are swimming behind them.

LESTER: Big party, was it?

(BARRY *has leant right over the back of Lester's chair, after a lap of the room, and, while talking, is examining the neat line of sheets which are spread out for each case on top of the desk in front of* LESTER.)

BARRY: It's like a small rodent has pissed in my mouth.
(*In fact everyone is working while this goes on, ignoring the suspects on the bench.* DAVE *is rifling through the woman's handbag.* LESTER *is filling in forms.*)

DAVE: Yes, well, it's possible. In the position you were in when I last saw you.

LESTER: Horizontal, was he?

BARRY: I was conducting an interview.

DAVE: Yeah. We saw. With the barmaid.
(BARRY *smiles across at* JIMMY.)

BARRY: English sense of humour.
(*He has taken off his glasses, and for the first time notices* SANDRA, *who is in his eyeline, showing* JIMMY *the bag of dope.*)

SANDRA: Will you take a look at this, Jimmy?

BARRY: Oh, it's you.

SANDRA: Good morning, Barry.

BARRY: I didn't see you.

SANDRA: No. (*She smiles and goes back to work.*) Well, I'm here.
(*The atmosphere changes subtly as* BARRY *goes back to examining the day's work.*)

BARRY: So what do we have?

LESTER: Sandra's brought in this body. Invoking his right to silence.

BARRY: That's good. It's your democratic right. That's what it's for. You use it.

LESTER: But there's a major procedural problem.
(JIMMY *has thrown the pack across the room to* BARRY, *who holds it up to look at it.*)

BARRY: Oh! Illegal substances.

LESTER: I can't fill in the form because he won't tell me his name.

KEITH: I'm not bloody talking. You're all bloody bastards.
(BARRY *looks at him a moment, then nods to* JIMMY.)

BARRY: I see. All right, get some tapes, will you Jimmy?

JIMMY: Happy to.
(JIMMY *goes to the drawer and gets tapes, which* LESTER *inspects and signs out.*)

BARRY: Because we have to interview you. On tape. That's the law of the land.

KEITH: If you bloody touch me, I'll have you. I'll get you for wrongful arrest.

(BARRY *is moving towards him, nodding.*)

JIMMY: Do you want a solicitor?

KEITH: I'm not saying anything.

JIMMY: What do you think, Lester, can we take that as no?

(BARRY *stands still for a moment, looking up at* KEITH. *Then he turns back and points at the* WOMAN.)

BARRY: All right, fair enough, we can do this one first.

(*The others laugh as* SANDRA *at once protests.*)

SANDRA: Oh, come on now, just wait a moment . . .

BARRY: All right.

SANDRA: I never understand it, you make an arrest, it takes precisely two minutes, you bring them in and you wait on average, on *average* four hours, that's half your relief . . .

LESTER: Yeah, yeah, we know it . . .

BARRY: Well, you know the answer.

DAVE: We all do. (*He looks up.*)

BARRY: It's simple. *Don't bring anyone in.*

(*He smiles triumphantly round the room. They are all smiling at* SANDRA's *familiar predicament.*)

I mean, come on, you boys, just think of it, if you never made any arrests, you'd all be out there on the streets all the time, and London would be so much better policed.

(*The police all look ironically at him. He is right by the bench on which the* WOMEN *are now sitting.*)

So what are we going to do? I don't know. I suppose we're going to sit here.

(*He sits down on the bench right next to the* WOMAN. *He ignores* KEITH *above him, on the other side.*)

Good morning, madam. I'm Barry. How are you?

WOMAN: All right.

BARRY: Well, good. Do I know you? Haven't you used us before?

WOMAN: Once or twice.

BARRY: I thought I'd seen you. Would you like a cup of coffee?

WOMAN: She wouldn't mind something to eat.

BARRY: Lester?

LESTER: Sure.

(*The woman's* FRIEND *has begun to cry again.* BARRY *looks up at* KEITH.)

BARRY: Sunshine? What about you?

(KEITH *doesn't answer.* DAVE *has checked through the handbag and is trying to give the credit cards to* LESTER.)

LESTER: Has someone nicked the light meal vouchers?

DAVE: At least we can do these. Can we do a check for stolen numbers?

LESTER: Oh, well, you're in luck, main meal vouchers. They'll just have to do.

(*The* WOMAN *looks round. The atmosphere is quietly industrious and cheerful.* BARRY *has a grin on his face, as if this hiatus is perfectly enjoyable.*)

WOMAN: Why are you lot so cheerful?

LESTER: Why are we cheerful? We're cheerful because Barry here had a bit of luck.

BARRY: What do you mean, 'luck'? (*He turns scornfully to the* WOMAN.) Don't believe it, darling. It wasn't luck.

DAVE: You see, he's a detective. And he finally managed to detect.

BARRY: Now that is a travesty. Here, ask Jimmy.

JIMMY: I'm not getting into this.

LESTER: Oh, Barry's getting shirty.

BARRY: I bloody well am.

LESTER: CID hates it when you call it luck. In uniform, you see, we don't mind admitting. We're sort of *grown-up* in that way.

BARRY: (*More insistently*) It wasn't luck.

(LESTER *is laughing as he writes.*)

LESTER: This is Barry's big triumph, yesterday he and Jimmy were at the Bailey – all right? – they got three pretty nasty villains put away. Only what they don't tell you is how they found them in the first place.

BARRY: All right, you go on, I don't mind, you say what you like.

(*He waves a hand at* LESTER *to continue. The* WOMAN *frowns.*)

WOMAN: How did you find them?

DAVE: By brilliant detection.

BARRY: All right . . .

LESTER: Meaning: there was this woman who actually ran out into the street at two o'clock in the morning, finds the patrolling officer, who happens to be Sandra . . .

SANDRA: That's right . . .

LESTER: Who happens – by chance – to be driving right by, and she says there's a very loud party. It's a 'celebration' or something

23

in the council flat right next to hers. And she can't get to sleep because the music's too loud . . .

SANDRA: I go in . . .

LESTER: Yeah, and on the floor, oh my goodness, there she sees three leather coats, identical . . .

BARRY: All right . . .

LESTER: And – hey! – a toolbag. So because she's quite bright, she leaves as if she's seen nothing, and goes and sits in her car. Sure enough, ten minutes later, they take the stuff down to a lock-up just behind the flat. (*He looks ironically at* BARRY.) So next morning in goes Hercule Poirot, into the lock-up, where he finds two hundred leather coats, then into the flat, with about six of us. And being a detective doesn't look too bloody hard.

BARRY: I'm not telling any of you what happens after.

DAVE: Why not, Barry?

BARRY: How you make the connections. How you actually connect the right people to the job. How you make the case watertight. How you see it through to court.

DAVE: How is that done, Barry?

BARRY: Through what is called the exercise of my professional skill.

(*They all laugh.*)

LESTER: Oh yeah, right, thank you . . .

DAVE: Yeah. I think we saw that last night.

LESTER: What, you mean with the barmaid?

(BARRY *smiles contentedly and then looks up at* KEITH *above him.*)

BARRY: What do you think, lad? Are you listening to this?

(*There's suddenly a moment's pause in all the kidding. When* KEITH *speaks, he's quite serious.*)

KEITH: I'll tell you what I think. The police are all tossers. You'd have to be a tosser to want to do the job.

BARRY: Yeah. You're right. That is probably true. (*He is wistful, as if now considering it.*) Or rather, people call you a tosser. I mean, look at Lester. He sits opposite that door. People call him names, maybe twenty times a day. You'd have to be a tosser to be able to put up with it. I mean, without showing you mind.

24

(*He smiles.* SANDRA *has stopped work, to listen, enjoying Barry's line of thought, smiling with him.*)

BARRY: Or perhaps you *don't* mind. Perhaps you stop caring. What would you say, Lester? Perhaps after a while you find you've taken so much shit that when people whinge about how they hate the police, you just think, fair enough . . . I'm not sure I care for the public that much.

(*He smiles.* LESTER *says nothing, knowing what* BARRY *is up to.* BARRY *does not even look up at* KEITH.)

Cuts both ways, doesn't it?

(*There is silence now in the charge room.*)

I'll tell you my idea of a tosser. He's someone who's been caught with a small piece of dope. The chances are he'll get off with a caution. Which if he had any nous he would know. But this one wants to get sent down for resisting arrest.

(*There's a pause.*)

KEITH: Did you say a caution?

BARRY: We haven't interviewed you yet.

(BARRY *is still not looking at him.*)

Name?

KEITH: Keith Machin.

BARRY: Age?

KEITH: Seventeen.

(LESTER *writes.*)

LESTER: Did you say she planted this on you?

(KEITH *pauses a second.*)

KEITH: No.

LESTER: Do you want a solicitor?

KEITH: No.

LESTER: Then sign here.

(KEITH *gets down from the bench to sign.* BARRY *takes no notice, as if it were inevitable.*)

BARRY: You'll take him, will you, Jimmy?

JIMMY: I will.

BARRY: What about these two?

LESTER: They're coming down with me. Get Esther, because we need to do a body search.

WOMAN: You're not looking up my whatsit.

LESTER: Madam, I most certainly am not.

(*He has gathered a big bunch of keys, which he now takes off down the corridor, leading the two* WOMEN, DAVE, TOBY *and* ESTHER *away with him.* BARRY *has got up.*)

KEITH: You promised me a caution.

BARRY: I didn't promise you. I mentioned it, all right? Now you get along and confess your heart out to Jimmy.

(BARRY *nods and reaches out, holding Keith's arm a moment.*)

All right, sunshine? And then we'll decide.

(JIMMY *and* KEITH *go.* BARRY *watches them a moment.*)

He could be my son. That's what I think. When I see the young ones. Not that I'd ever know. Since his mother ran off with the antiques dealer from Cheltenham.

(*He turns and smiles at* SANDRA.)

I wonder, do they choose them deliberately to insult you?

SANDRA: No. That's just how it seems.

(*They both smile.*)

BARRY: How are you?

SANDRA: You seem well.

BARRY: Sure. I mean, there's got to be some satisfaction, hasn't there, in this job?

(*They smile.*)

The Crown Prosecution Service didn't lose the papers. The witnesses actually turned up. There was no psychiatrist to say their mothers never gave them the tit. Three men were actually sent down for a crime they committed. (*He shakes his head.*) Heavens to Betsy, we got a result.

SANDRA: Well done.

BARRY: I glimpsed you in the corridor. Outside the court, last day of the trial. Even there you were studying.

SANDRA: Naturally. I'm going on a course.

BARRY: Yes. I'm sure you are.

(*They both smile.*)

When you die, you know, there's a fork in the road with two pathways. One leads straight to heaven, that's where most people go. But to policemen they say, would you prefer the road marked 'Courses for *preparing* for heaven'? And do you know over half the coppers say yes?

(*She laughs. He has moved over and sat on the edge of the desk. She hasn't moved.*)

26

SANDRA: What you did just now, with the boy . . .

BARRY: Yeah.

SANDRA: It made me laugh. That was textbook.

BARRY: Sure.

SANDRA: Divert attention with some stories. Do everything you can to take the pressure off.

BARRY: Yes, that's right. (*He smiles.*) Then you throw the golden bridge. I love it.

SANDRA: (*Quoting from memory*) 'The suspect must believe he has a means of escape.'

BARRY: (*Shrugs*) Doesn't often work, I tell you.

SANDRA: So you must be getting lucky?

BARRY: Yeah, it's true. I'm on a streak. I'd been after that lot.

SANDRA: Did you know them?

BARRY: Sure. What, Travis and Faulkner? Yes, of course I knew them. As it happens I'd known them for years.

(SANDRA *frowns.*)

SANDRA: You knew them?

BARRY: Yes.

SANDRA: Then why didn't you say so?

BARRY: Didn't I?

(*She turns away, disbelieving.*)

SANDRA: Barry, you astonish me.

BARRY: Why?

SANDRA: Because when we all went in with the search warrant, you never gave the slightest sign you'd met them before.

BARRY: No. (*He shrugs, trying to turn it away.*) Well, there was no point. We knew they'd done a load of other jobs.

SANDRA: How did you know that?

BARRY: How? In the way you do. You just *know*. But because we'd never been able to stick those jobs on them, we decided to let them go by.

(SANDRA *is shaking her head.*)

SANDRA: You never even mentioned it. In all the months afterwards. In all the time you were preparing the case.

BARRY: Haven't I? Oh really?

(*He is looking blankly at her.*)

SANDRA: Did you know all of them?

BARRY: I knew Travis and Faulkner.

27

SANDRA: What about McKinnon?

BARRY: No. No, actually. McKinnon was new.

(*His tone is thoughtful for a moment, and* SANDRA *responds to the doubt in his voice.*)

SANDRA: I wasn't sure if he was guilty.

BARRY: Of course he was guilty. Forensic linked him to the stuff, and to the van.

SANDRA: So he sat outside?

BARRY: Most likely. Yes. He was the driver, wasn't he?

SANDRA: And he wasn't there when the guard was tied up?

BARRY: No.

SANDRA: But he got five years?

BARRY: Yeah.

SANDRA: For a first offence? I suppose I'm asking, did that surprise you?

BARRY: He lied. That didn't help him. Let's face it, he told a pack of lies. What's more, he was sort of, well, what's the word? He was kind of *Irish* as well.

(*He smiles, but* SANDRA *pursues it.*)

SANDRA: He isn't Irish, he's British.

BARRY: Oh, very funny. He may happen to hail from the North. But he did stand with a load of Micks outside the Irish pub on Clapham Common every evening. I think we can guess his primary allegiance.

SANDRA: And you're saying judges take that into account?

(BARRY *shakes his head.*)

BARRY: Oh, leave it out, Sandra, you're not just out of Hendon.

SANDRA: I'm asking.

BARRY: You're not in the Dream Palace now.

SANDRA: I'm not being stupid, that's why I'm asking. Come on, you're meant to have some sort of heavyweight experience, are you really telling me that's how judges' minds work?

(BARRY *tries to be as firm as he can.*)

BARRY: Sandra, we are talking about a body of men who sometimes choose to go to work dressed in stockings and suspenders. I'm buggered if I know how their bloody minds work.

SANDRA: All right, all right . . .

(BARRY *is shaking his head, insistent.*)

28

BARRY: Darling, you do have to deal with that. I'm not being funny. Next time you're tempted to be serious when you look at a judge. Under the robes. Under the language. Under the gravity. Please remember: he has made a style choice for which any adult male except Danny La Rue would be instantly arrested.

SANDRA: And is that why a man with an Irish accent gets such a bad deal?

(BARRY *looks at her, squaring with her now.*)

BARRY: All right, look, they don't *know* they're prejudiced. That's not how they think of it. It's like when I do an interview, I've never turned round and said, 'You black bastard.' But when I come out, I can't help it, I always feel virtuous because I *haven't* said it. It's like you've done them a favour. You actually start thinking, oh, I must be a really nice bloke. (*He nods.*) And that was my take on what happened yesterday. I know it. I've seen it so many times. The judge thought, I'm being nice, I'm being decent, I'm giving him less than the others. In *spite* of the fact that he's Irish.

SANDRA: He isn't. He isn't Irish.

BARRY: God, you're stubborn.

SANDRA: I know.

(*She smiles.* BARRY *has sat down on the desk beside her.*)

It's just, you know . . . I did get a sight of him. I got a sight of this bloke.

BARRY: And? What?

(*She shakes her head, slightly embarrassed.*)

No, I'd like to hear it, please tell me.

SANDRA: The fact is, he's just a lad.

BARRY: But that's none of our business.

SANDRA: He's got a very young family.

BARRY: So?

(SANDRA *is uneasy now, shifting away.*)

So?

SANDRA: It's silly. You think . . . you know, what's our job? Scrotes and dickheads, that's what everyone tells you. (*She smiles, making a joke of it.*) I told you, my family's been full of police . . .

BARRY: Your Dad . . .
SANDRA: That's right . . .
(*She looks at him a moment.*)
I mean, yeah, my Dad for a start. So it's always been the same.
And by and large, they're right. Fair enough. I don't see
things differently. They warned me. You choose our
profession, it's scrotes and dickheads all day. (*She pauses a
second.*) But what do you do when you bring in one who isn't?
(BARRY *laughs.*)
BARRY: Oh, what, and the nice ones shouldn't go down?
SANDRA: No . . .
BARRY: That's the ultimate snobbery. There should be a sort of
test! What, the niceness defence? Yes, your Honour, my
client did do it, he did it, but you should see him, he's magic
with children and animals. (*He turns away.*) Just lock them
up, Sandra, and get on with your job. We're not playing God.
(*She shakes her head, not taking him seriously.*)
SANDRA: Why do you pretend?
BARRY: Pretend?
SANDRA: Yes. Acting heartless.
BARRY: I'm not acting. I am.
SANDRA: You know that's not true.
BARRY: Isn't it?
SANDRA: No. No, it isn't. Not when we're alone.
BARRY: Oh *well* . . . that's different.
(*They both smile.*)
SANDRA: Any more than you've ever looked at a barmaid in your
life.
BARRY: Oh, that.
SANDRA: Yes.
(*She has moved away to a filing cabinet to catch up on her
paperwork.* BARRY *is still on the desk, laughing now.*)
BARRY: Well, you have to do all that, don't you? If you're a copper,
I mean. You've got to *be* a copper. It's expected. You have to
give it lots of mouth. Talk about how you go over the side. If
you say, oh, I just went home, had a Lucozade and thought
about Sandra, you're letting the boys down. (*He smiles at her.*)
Didn't they tell you? It's a team game.
SANDRA: No. No one mentioned it. (*She carries on working,*

consulting a file.) You know how vicars on trains are meant to carry *Playboy*. Only they have to cover it, so people don't see, with a copy of Proust. But coppers put Proust inside their *Playboy*.

BARRY: Proust? Is that that Swedish furniture store on the North Circular?

SANDRA: Oh sure, yeah. I expect you've bloody read it.

BARRY: He eats a biscuit, is that right?

SANDRA: You know perfectly well. You think it's clever to pretend to be stupid.

(*He looks at her a moment. Her back is turned to him*.)

BARRY: In this job, sometimes it is.

(*She catches his tone and turns directly to him*.)

SANDRA: Why didn't you say? If you already knew them? Why didn't you mention it?

BARRY: Oh. I didn't want anyone to know. It's clearer that way. It's simpler. I like a clear pond. Not muddy.

(SANDRA'*s gaze doesn't waver*.)

SANDRA: So you lied?

BARRY: What? (*He leans forward, his ear cupped*.) I didn't hear you. What was that word? 'Lied'? It's not in my vocabulary. Do we have a dictionary? I'll just look it up.

(*She smiles*.)

SANDRA: And them?

BARRY: What?

SANDRA: No, it's something else that puzzles me. I mean, OK, I can see you decided to pretend not to recognize them. You've explained it. I sort of understand.

BARRY: Well?

(BARRY *stands, frowning slightly, waiting for her to go on*.)

SANDRA: That bit's easy. But the problem is, Barry . . . You see what I'm asking . . . Why did they pretend not to know you? (*She frowns. There is a sudden silence. The atmosphere has changed. Before* BARRY *can answer,* LESTER *comes hurrying back to go to a cupboard to look for something*.)

LESTER: Jeez Louise, it's one of those mornings. Esther can't find any gloves.

SANDRA: Gloves?

LESTER: For the body search.

(BARRY *has not moved. He is standing quite still in the middle of the room, as* DAVE *now returns.*)

DAVE: Did you want to see me, Sergeant?

LESTER: Dave, they just had a call. It's a sudden death.
(*He turns at the cupboard and hands a quickly scrawled note to* DAVE. *As he does he frowns at* BARRY *and* SANDRA.) What are you two doing? Sandra, wasting your time?

SANDRA: Yes, Sarge, you got it.
(*She moves to pull her coat and hat on.* DAVE *is very slowly putting on his gloves.*)
What about him? Shouldn't he be hurrying?

DAVE: Hardly. If it's a sudden death, it doesn't make any difference when I turn up.
(JIMMY *comes back from the cells impatiently.*)

JIMMY: Where are you, Barry? You on strike or something?

BARRY: Yeah, of course. I'm just on my way.

LESTER: He's still dreaming of the barmaid.

BARRY: Oh yeah, naturally.

LESTER: Are you going to tell us what she's actually like?
(*He has collected the gloves and is now doing some quick form-hunting.* DAVE *and* SANDRA *are both dressing to go out.* JIMMY *has moved to a filing cabinet to check records.*)

BARRY: Oh, extraordinary. She's really something. Don't you think so, Sandra?

SANDRA: How would I know?

BARRY: She can dial a telephone with her nipples.
(LESTER *at once carries the Standing Orders book to another filing cabinet to look for another form.*)

LESTER: Yeah, we get the picture, thanks very much.
(SANDRA *looks ironically across the busy room at the departing* BARRY.)

SANDRA: Does she go all night, then, Barry?

BARRY: All night, Sandra.

SANDRA: That must be nice.

BARRY: In its way. You know, I mean, sure. But men are funny.
(*She looks at him briefly.*)
Give them too much, it still isn't enough.
(*He makes to go but, before he can,* TOBY *comes back from the cells, urgently.*)

32

TOBY: There's a pub fight, Sarge. Two scrotes in the Windmill tearing each other apart. (*He turns to* JIMMY.) And your body's throwing his chair round the room.

(JIMMY *dashes off to collect the keys and runs down the corridor. Meanwhile, from the other door, uniformed police are coming in, ready-dressed, to go to the pub fight.* JIMMY *nearly bumps into* ESTHER *coming from the cells.*)

BARRY: Go for it, Jimmy.

ESTHER: Is anyone coming? I've got two naked women weeping and no bloody gloves.

(DAVE *turns at the main door, Rambo-like. The stage is suddenly full of blue serge.*)

DAVE: We're all going out.

LESTER: Yeah.

DAVE: Fighting crime.

(*There is just a second's suspension.* SANDRA *smiles.*)

SANDRA: Let's get them before they get us.

SCENE SIX

As the police disperse, the stage expands and BECKETT *leads* IRINA *through the wire-fenced courtyard that leads to the huge wing of the gaol. They are two small figures walking gingerly through the vast area.* IRINA *is smartly dressed, in coat and good shoes.*

BECKETT: All right, it's this way. (*As they approach, he points to the ground.*) Watch the shit packages.

IRINA: Oh yes. Goodness.

BECKETT: The prisoners throw them out of their windows.

IRINA: Yes, yes, I see.

(*He lets her into the main well of the prison block. At once, the stage darkens, with the high criss-cross light cutting through the Victorian gloom.*)

Thank you.

(*There is a single, scrubby table and two metal chairs with canvas seats.*)

Well, it's some sort of protest?

BECKETT: No. It's not a protest. No, it's more they don't like the

33

smell.

(BECKETT *moves round the room to arrange the table and chairs for her.*)

Have you been here before?

IRINA: No. Not to this one.

BECKETT: We get a lot of visitors . . .

IRINA: I'm sure.

BECKETT: Coming to look over this place. We have a name for them.

IRINA: Oh yes. What's that?

BECKETT: We call them Something-Must-Be-Dones. Oh, look, we say, there's another bunch of Something-Must-Be-Dones. (*He looks around.*) This place is their monument.

IRINA: And is nothing done?

(*He looks at her a moment, a sudden, quiet flash of real feeling.*)

BECKETT: Only by us, Miss Platt. It's left to us.

IRINA: Yes.

(*He looks her straight in the eye.*)

BECKETT: Still, I think the prisoners like it. Or why else do they keep coming back?

(*GERARD has appeared. The three of them stand a moment, silent in the vast area. GERARD is a little ghostly, more suited to his clothes now, which he has found a way of tucking in, but grey and still.*)

McKinnon?

GERARD: Yes?

BECKETT: This lady's come to see you. It's all yours. You can have as long as you like.

(*BECKETT turns and goes. GERARD does not move. IRINA hovers nervously by the table.*)

IRINA: This is kind. It's good of you to see me.

(*There is no reply.*)

I wonder, did your solicitor mention I'd be here?

GERARD: No.

(*IRINA nods and sits down. GERARD is watching her all the time.*)

But then it's not very likely.

IRINA: Why's that?

GERARD: I don't know him very well.

34

(*There's a pause.*)

IRINA: Uh-huh.

GERARD: When he took me on as a client, he actually handed me a pen. It said, 'Trust me, I'm a solicitor.'

(IRINA *smiles, relieved he's talking.*)

To be honest, I haven't seen much of him since.

IRINA: No.

GERARD: There was a pen I'd seen which I wanted to give him in return. But it was too late.

IRINA: Oh yes. What did that say?

GERARD: I saw it once, in a shop by the seaside. It said, 'Don't jerk me off, I've already come.'

IRINA: Yes. (*She readjusts a little.*) Yes, well I can see why you feel that.

GERARD: I don't mean to use dirty words.

IRINA: No, it's all right. I'm used to them. I'm also used to anti-lawyer jokes. People don't like us. They think we're taxi-meters. Tick tick tick.

GERARD: Am I paying for this?

IRINA: No. No, certainly not. But I think we should establish just what 'this' is.

(GERARD *is standing mistrustfully, exactly where he was when he came in.*)

I've got a proposition. It's purely my own. I haven't run it by Sir Peter.

GERARD: Why not?

IRINA: He takes a different view. And I have to say he's much more experienced than me. The judges are his friends. They all eat together. (*She smiles.*) But I think you should be considering an appeal.

GERARD: Ah.

IRINA: Yes. Against the length of your sentence. It seemed to me harsh.

GERARD: It seems harsh to me.

IRINA: If you were just the driver. The question is, of course, why you denied the whole thing. Perhaps if you'd pleaded guilty . . . Did you ever consider that?

(GERARD *waits.*)

GERARD: It's hard.

IRINA: Why is it hard?
  (GERARD *doesn't answer*.)
  You mean because of the others?
  (GERARD *doesn't look at her*.)
  Perhaps you should talk to me first about them.
  (GERARD *shifts a little*.)
GERARD: I really can't say.
IRINA: You see, my feeling is, this is just instinct, while I
  watched you, I thought you were in fear. And so you'd
  probably done what they asked you.
  (*He is impassive*.)
GERARD: I can't say anything.
IRINA: No. No, I see.
  (*They have reached an apparent impasse. Quietly,* IRINA *diverts
  in another direction*.)
  How is it here? How are the conditions?
  (GERARD *looks at her as if the question doesn't need answering*.)
  Are you going to manage all right?
GERARD: I tried to take a course, you know. There's a
  bookbinding course. I thought, that's interesting. It takes
  four weeks. You learn how to do it. But then you can't
  practise until you get out.
IRINA: That's absurd.
GERARD: Yes. They give you something. Then they take it away.
  (GERARD *suddenly looks right through her, an unexpected
  darkness in him. He still has not moved*.)
  There's three in my cell. I don't want to do what the other
  two are doing all day.
IRINA: What's that?
GERARD: I won't say . . . in front of you.
  (IRINA *looks down*.)
  I can't stand watching them. I've only been here a week.
IRINA: Can't you ask to be moved?
GERARD: Would it be any better?
IRINA: It might be.
GERARD: Do you know the procedure?
IRINA: I don't. I could find out.
GERARD: Why don't you know?
IRINA: Why?

GERARD: Yes.

IRINA: I'm just a lawyer. (*She hesitates a moment, then smiles.*) We say goodbye to you when you go through the court's doors. (*He nods.*)

GERARD: Is that a good thing?

IRINA: It's the system. We're all in different compartments. The judges used to visit the prisons in the old days. But now they say it affects their independence. If they knew what the prisoner was in for, it might affect their judgement.

GERARD: Yes. (*He nods, for the first time beginning to loosen up.*) Too right it would.

IRINA: They say it isn't their problem.

GERARD: And you're going to make your life with these guys? (IRINA *nods, still smiling.*)

IRINA: Yes. As it happens.

GERARD: Good luck to you.

IRINA: Why not? There are good reasons. If you think about this country, what do they do well? They're good at thatching cottages. They serve brilliant cream teas. They're the best gardeners in the world. Oh yes, and one other thing, it's a real talent they have . . . (*She smiles.*) They send more people to prison than practically anyone else in Europe. (GERARD *smiles, intrigued by her now.*)

GERARD: Is that so? Is that really so?

IRINA: Do you know how many men of your age are convicted of a crime?

GERARD: No.

IRINA: One in three.

GERARD: Oh, really?

IRINA: Yes. (GERARD *laughs.*)

GERARD: And you mean that's just the ones who they catch?

IRINA: Well, exactly. So add in the ones who are getting away with it. Then add to those the ones that aren't reported at all. Criminality of one sort or another is well-nigh universal among young men between eighteen and thirty. Until they abandon it from what's called inertia. Which is another word for marriage. They get married and then they stop doing it . . .

37

(*They both smile.*)
Or maybe they decide the nights are too cold . . . (*She is assured now, at ease.*) So the sensible thing would be to say, OK, being a criminal's an adolescent phase, it's like wearing an ear-ring or listening to pop, it's mildly annoying but it won't last for long. But oh no. We're too self-righteous for that. We get on our high horses and say, let's send them all to a university where they can acquire all the attitudes they need to turn them into criminals for life.

GERARD: You feel pretty strongly. (*He frowns a moment.*) Is this how you are all the time?

IRINA: No. (*She smiles slightly, but without backing down.*) And I know it's no use to you.

GERARD: No, I'm not meaning that.

IRINA: I'm sorry. It's your case we're discussing, we're here to talk about you . . .

GERARD: I'm finding it quite a relief.

IRINA: Are you sure?

GERARD: Yes.
(*They both smile now, the contact suddenly easy between them.*) What do you think I do all day? I go over and over the things that I've done. You know I've got two little ones?

IRINA: Yes.

GERARD: They're aged two and one. I think about them all the time. How they are. How Barbara's coping.
(IRINA *waits, silent now.*)
Do you have any idea what that's like?

IRINA: No. (*She thinks a moment.*) No, I can't imagine.

GERARD: You go back all the time. Go back and examine everything you did. Why you did the job.

IRINA: I see. (*She is still gentle, but a touch more formal now.*) So you did do it?
(*He looks at her.*)

GERARD: And why I lied.

IRINA: Why did you lie?

GERARD: 'Cos I'm scared. Scared, so I have to go to the lavatory. That sort of scared, do you know?
(*She smiles.*)

IRINA: Yes.

GERARD: Have you known that?

IRINA: Just . . . No, it's silly . . .

(*She stops, embarrassed.*)

GERARD: Tell me.

IRINA: Once. When I was in love.

GERARD: Oh, really?

IRINA: Sure. When I thought of him. When I thought, oh, I'll see him today. Or tonight. Or I thought, I may lose him. My stomach turned over. (*She is taken aback a moment at the intimacy between them.*) I know it's not the same thing.

(GERARD *is now looking at her intently.*)

GERARD: Are you in love now?

IRINA: This was in Antigua.

GERARD: Is that where you're from?

(*She nods.*)

So are British men a let-down in comparison?

IRINA: I think we're straying right off the path.

GERARD: I know, but it's great.

(*He smiles, still looking at her, making her answer.*)

IRINA: To answer you . . . No. It's more . . . It's just difficult now, having known the real thing. Anything less, so to speak, seems sort of pointless. (*She smiles.*) People always tell me I'm unrealistic. Not just about love. In everything. They say all or nothing's no way to live.

(GERARD *has turned and is looking at her thoughtfully.*)

But so many people seem to settle for so little.

GERARD: Maybe. Maybe most people don't have a choice.

(*There is a darkness in his tone which she catches, then looks down.*)

IRINA: Yes.

(GERARD *looks at her, as if making a silent pact. Then he speaks quietly, released.*)

GERARD: I came over, you know, I got the boat to Holyhead only two years ago. I hitch-hiked down the M1. That very first day, I was on that corner in Cricklewood. You know that corner?

IRINA: I do.

GERARD: You get a day's labouring, if you get there early. The vans come by, they pick you up about six.

39

IRINA: What happened to that?

GERARD: It was all the big houses, being refurbished. I saw some great houses. Then there was the slump.

IRINA: Yes.

GERARD: And I'd met a girl. (*He stops for a moment.*)

IRINA: Well, that's great.

GERARD: Yes, it is. Then she was pregnant, so I got a job as a hospital porter. But we could only get a room above a pub. The noise was just dreadful. And the first child . . . (*He hesitates.*) Perhaps you've heard this . . . Well, the child wasn't right.

IRINA: No.

(*She has relaxed now, at ease with him at last.*)

GERARD: The pub is a little bit Republican, so there's a lot of singing. It can go on till four. So I started driving. We needed the money.

IRINA: At nights?

GERARD: Yes. To get stuff to the market.

IRINA: When did you sleep?

GERARD: When I got to the hospital. I'd kip in the laundry room. There were nurses who liked me.

IRINA: I can see why they would.

(*But GERARD is too absorbed now to notice what she says.*)

GERARD: I was thinking, you know, it's like the water's up to here . . . (*He draws a line across his neck.*) One big wave and I'm gone. Every week I just about survive and no more. Then Barbara was pregnant again. I was asked to do this job, I thought, OK, just the once. What everyone needs is one lump of money. And the waves will only be up to my chest. (*He stands a moment, thinking.*)

IRINA: How much were you to get?

GERARD: Oh, not 'all or nothing' . . .

IRINA: No . . .

(*She smiles, acknowledging the phrase.*)

GERARD: They don't give you the moon. Eight hundred. It's tempting. (*He thinks again a moment.*) It's pretty hard to say no.

(IRINA *takes out her notebook and lays it on the desk, not yet writing.*)

IRINA: How did you first know Travis and Faulkner?

GERARD: I'd met them in the pub. Then they'd got in touch. The whole thing was terribly simple. And I sat outside in the van, shit-scared, I admit. Then they came running out. Off we went. They didn't even mention the bloke they'd tied up. (*He shrugs.*) I went home, you understand. I thought, that was easy. But I hadn't been paid. This was three days after the job. I went round to Faulkner's place. It was bad luck. (*He hesitates a moment.*) We were just talking and in came the police. They had a warrant. They were going to search the flat.

IRINA: Did they?

GERARD: Oh, sure. They went into the bathroom. Then after a moment there, they came out. (*He stops.*) They had a bag of white stuff.

IRINA: White stuff? (*She frowns.*) And how did Travis and Faulkner react?

GERARD: They weren't surprised.

IRINA: Are you sure?

GERARD: It didn't surprise them. Faulkner just looked at it and said, 'Oh, I thought you might find something like that.' (*IRINA has begun to write now.*)
Then they looked at me. The detective said he thought I should leave.

IRINA: So who stayed behind?

GERARD: Just the two others. And the copper himself. (*IRINA thinks a moment.*)

IRINA: So did you then get in touch with Travis and Faulkner?

GERARD: Well, sure, of course. I was going crazy. I called them, I said, look, I saw in that bag. Tell me if I'm in way over my head. They said, calm down, it was a stitch-up. It wasn't drugs, it was aspirin. Powdered aspirin.

IRINA: Who powders aspirin?

GERARD: That's what I said. (*He looks at her a moment.*)
Then they said, 'Look, when we're arrested, we've decided we're pleading not guilty. You need an alibi.' I said, 'No, I don't want to do that. Thinking up stories, perjuring witnesses.' They said, 'We're telling you.'

IRINA: They threatened you?

GERARD: Yes.

(*He looks at her.*)

They said they could get to me. They said in the past they'd used guns.

IRINA: Did you believe them?

GERARD: They mentioned Barbara.

(*He has stopped.* IRINA *discreetly stops writing.*)

If it was just me, I'd have risked it. Why not? But it wasn't just me.

(*He stops, overwhelmed.* IRINA *is thoughtful, quiet now.*)

IRINA: Gerard, I'm sorry, you know, I'm trying to understand you . . .

GERARD: I know.

IRINA: I'm listening to everything you say . . .

GERARD: I know. But you've got a problem. (*He smiles.*) The whole thing doesn't make sense.

(*She frowns and leans in across the table to him.*)

IRINA: The police had called at the flat . . .

GERARD: Yes . . .

IRINA: They'd called earlier that night, to ask them to turn the music down . . .

GERARD: Yes . . .

IRINA: So Faulkner *knew*, he cleared all the goods down to the lock-up because he knew the police might well appear again . . .

(GERARD *nods.*)

GERARD: That's right.

IRINA: So that means the police must have planted the bag. But for what? For a deal? Is that it? But what deal? (*She waits a moment.*) Gerard?

(*He has turned away, not seeming to hear her for a moment. Then he turns back.*)

GERARD: I'm afraid I have no idea.

(*There is barely a moment, and then a bell rings. They both start. As they have been talking, evening has arrived. They are both left with only high, grey light above them.*)

What's that?

GERARD: It's tea. It's tea and recreation.

(IRINA *looks round, suddenly conscious of their isolation.*)

IRINA: My God, it's dark. They've forgotten us.

(*She looks at him, two people embarrassed at finding themselves alone.*)

I must go. We should find someone. (*She gets up.*) May I come back? May I come back tomorrow?

GERARD: Yes, I'd like that.

IRINA: Good. So would I.

(*He is still seated, not moving, reluctant to let the moment go.*)

What do you do?

GERARD: Do?

IRINA: I mean now.

(*He smiles.*)

GERARD: Now? I have tea and go back to my cell.

(*She looks at him for a moment.*)

IRINA: I shouldn't say this. It's irresponsible. They teach you at college you must never do this. But you do have a friend now. I promise you.

(GERARD *doesn't move.*)

Keep faith and I will. (*She looks down.*) I'll be in touch.

SCENE SEVEN

IRINA *goes, very quietly, leaving* GERARD *sitting alone, staring. The lights on the stage change in silence, isolating* GERARD, *then at the other side of the stage finding* BARRY, *also staring out, his work desk untidy and overflowing in front of him, a night-light burning on his desk, the empty police station behind him.*

The two men stare identically outwards, as in a dream.

Then, very distantly, the first chords of the overture of The Magic Flute, *just heard, and* JIMMY, *silent, sharp-suited, steps like a ghost in immediately behind* BARRY. BARRY *doesn't turn.*

BARRY: Oh, it's you, Jimmy.

(*He lifts a letter from the top of the desk and, without turning, hands it to* JIMMY, *who reads it.*)

JIMMY: So it's come.

BARRY: Yes.

43

JIMMY: You were expecting it.

BARRY: Not this soon.

JIMMY: They had to do it. Congratulations.

BARRY: I'm not sure I want it. I'm not sure I want to go without you.

(JIMMY *frowns, disbelieving*.)

JIMMY: Oh, come on now, Barry . . .

BARRY: Policing's all to do with your partner.

JIMMY: You've got to go.

BARRY: Have I?

JIMMY: The Flying Squad? Sure.

(JIMMY, *confident, steps forward*, BARRY *still not turning*.)
They owe you, Barry. You'll go. You're all policeman. You're the real thing.

(*At the other side of the stage*, BECKETT *has stepped in beside* GERARD, *equally ghost-like, equally unobserved*. JIMMY *and* BARRY *hold where they are. The overture continues, eerily, in the background*.)

BECKETT: You all right, McKinnon?

GERARD: Yes, I'm fine, thank you.

BECKETT: You've missed your tea.

(GERARD *turns, still in his dream*.)
We've lost you, I can tell. I know when it happens. For the next three months you're gone.

GERARD: Gone?

BECKETT: You'll be in Dreamland. They all go to Dreamland. You've got that vacant look on your face. For a while. They all get it. (*He smiles directly at* GERARD.) Did someone say something about an appeal?

(*Before* GERARD *can answer*, BARRY, *sitting back in his chair, smiles and starts talking. The Mozart continues*.)

BARRY: It's funny, you know, just lately, sitting in traffic, I find myself thinking, how long have I got? How long before it wears me right down? I have a fantasy, I'll walk right out of it . . . (*He smiles*.) Or shall I wait till they kick me out?

(*At once, again, before* JIMMY *can answer*, BECKETT *moves in towards* GERARD, *shaking his head; the music building a little now*.)

BECKETT: Look, did that lawyer tell you it was terrible? Did she

44

say a terrible injustice had been done? (*He gestures round the place.*) And how awful this prison is? (*He smiles.*) Then what did she do? I'll tell you. She walked away. Walk in. Upset them. Leave them. That's lawyers.

(GERARD *stands up and moves to the door, very quiet and calm.*)

GERARD: I believe in her. I think she's all right.

(*And, as he says this, the Mozart suddenly catches fire, the violins kicking into the* Allegro, *and the whole stage expands as* SIR PETER *and* IRINA, *the two of them in evening dress, walk up the main staircase towards the Crush Bar at the Royal Opera House.*)

SIR PETER: So you changed your mind about opera? Woody didn't seem to think it would interest you at all.

IRINA: Where did he get that idea? Goodness. How dare he?

SIR PETER: I was shocked. I thought I must be losing touch. I thought all educated young women loved music.

(IRINA *smiles.*)

IRINA: Yes, well, at the right moment, we do.

(*They stop at the top of the stairs. She turns her back to him.*) Take my coat off.

SIR PETER: I'm sorry?

IRINA: Take my coat off.

(SIR PETER *hesitates a second, then he takes the coat from her back. Underneath she is bare-armed in a full-length evening dress. For a moment neither of them says anything.*) All right?

SIR PETER: Yes. (*He hesitates, for once wrong-footed.*) Yes, fine.

IRINA: I wanted to ask you, I needed a word about Gerard McKinnon.

SIR PETER: McKinnon? Did you? Well, if you wish.

(*At this point,* GERARD *returns to his cell. He sits down on the edge of his bed, a thoughtful expression on his face.* BARRY *looks across at* JIMMY. *The stage is now divided into three: the Opera House, the police station and the cell.*)

JIMMY: Come on, Barry, cheer up.

(SIR PETER *smiles and leans in towards* IRINA, *pointing to some of the crowd in the Crush Bar.*)

SIR PETER: Do you know Sir Hamish Tyrone over there?

IRINA: No.

45

SIR PETER: He's the Cabinet Secretary. That's the Lord Chief. You know him, of course. And that's Lady Benenden, you've probably read about her.

IRINA: Tell me, I'd like to draw on your experience, do you understand? If you run the country, is it compulsory to go to the opera in the evening?

(SIR PETER *smiles, enjoying himself.*)

SIR PETER: You tell me. I have no idea.

(GERARD *turns a moment, as if hearing something. In the other part of the stage,* JIMMY *stirs, trying to reach* BARRY, *who is staring gloomily into space.*)

JIMMY: You're always saying it's impossible. You claim it's all over. You say it's all a lost art. But we did it last week.

BARRY: Just. By the skin of our teeth.

JIMMY: Yeah. But we did it. And that's what the whole thing's about.

(SIR PETER *and* IRINA, *carrying their programmes, move on down towards us.*)

IRINA: Well, what's your answer?

SIR PETER: Shall we talk over dinner?

IRINA: Which way are you leaning? Just an indication. If you tell me, I'll enjoy the opera much more.

(SIR PETER *thinks a moment, serious.*)

SIR PETER: You know as well as I do, the young man did everything wrong. He damned his own character. He told a complete pack of lies. He persisted in them long after he should. I don't have to tell you the Appeal Court will be starkly prejudiced against him. (*He pauses. Then he's quiet.*) But if you want me to, I'll take it on.

(*They stand a moment.* IRINA *smiles. As she does,* BECKETT *and two other screws patrol down the corridor outside the cells. All areas begin to move at once.*)

BARRY: Shall we get a drink?

SIR PETER: Is there time for a drink?

BECKETT: Lights out! Lights out!

(*The lights start to go out in the prison.*)

BARRY: Let's have a frame of snooker.

JIMMY: Great.

SIR PETER: This way.

(*As they start to move off,* BARRY *smiles easily at* JIMMY.)

BARRY: Oh, by the way, will you keep quiet about the Flying
Squad?

JIMMY: Surely.

BARRY: Just for now. Keep it to yourself.

(*They both grin.* BARRY *is standing directly opposite* JIMMY *and
now he puts his hands on his shoulders.*)

A man's got to have some secrets. Hasn't he?

(*The two men embrace.* SIR PETER *and* IRINA *take their seats.*)

JIMMY: Aren't you meant to call Sandra?

BARRY: Sandra? Who's Sandra?

(*The two men head off, arm in arm.*)

Come on, let's get out of here.

(IRINA *turns to* SIR PETER.)

IRINA: The opera's starting. I'm ready for this.

BECKETT: Lights out! Lights out!

(*The curtain rises. The opening chords of the first act ring out.*)

ACT TWO

SCENE ONE

The prison at night. Around the cell, the whole space of the prison is only dimly lit. The few fugitive figures in the darkness are some warders, sitting about in the far distance. GERARD *is in his cell, looking up to the small grey square of light above him at the cell window.*

GERARD: Six o'clock is the worst, that's when it hits you. When you sense the evening outside. Listening to the traffic. You were served your supper at four thirty. And now you're being told it's the end of the day. (*He pauses for a moment.*) Calm down, Gerard. Don't get excited. Each day I watch the evening come down. Just the grey, stretched like a tent over London. And the rain. And the smell of the kitchens, waiting for tomorrow. (*He is still.*) Oh God, let me not give in to hope.

SCENE TWO

At once, as if in response to Gerard, the sound of laughter, and judges and barristers murmuring in anticipation. We are in Lincoln's Inn. In a panelled ante-room, the guests are gathering, all in white tie and tails, for a formal dinner in the Hall. The High Table is visible beyond, in the Hall itself, laid out magnificently, with each place marked by four different wine glasses. The Inn's best silver is on display. Candles burn.

Here in the room in front a massively distinguished group is already forming, each guest announced on entry. CUDDEFORD, *wearing tails, is moving across to welcome a tall, balding man, apparently genial, in his fifties, who is just arriving.*

TOASTMASTER: The Home Secretary – the Right Honourable Kevin Cumberland MP.
(*Before he has a moment, the* HOME SECRETARY *finds* CUDDEFORD *beside him.*)

48

CUDDEFORD: Home Secretary, welcome. We are honoured to have you here.

HOME SECRETARY: Thank you.

CUDDEFORD: For one of our grand nights. You are guest of honour, of course.

HOME SECRETARY: You don't need to say that. In such distinguished company. What do I see? An ex-Prime Minister, an earl and a high commissioner?

(*He looks round the group where an African politician in tribal robes is notably resplendent. A number of the men are wearing medals.*)

CUDDEFORD: Yes. We've been trawling.

HOME SECRETARY: Indeed.

TOASTMASTER: The Governor of the Bank of England.

CUDDEFORD: With a rather fine net. (*He smiles at the* HOME SECRETARY.) We knew the law was not in your background.

HOME SECRETARY: No. No, I was an accountant.

CUDDEFORD: Yes, well, that's right. So we thought you might like to drink in the atmosphere, so that you were more fully informed.

HOME SECRETARY: Well, thank you.

CUDDEFORD: So you'd have some real, human faces in your mind when it comes to making vital decisions.

HOME SECRETARY: Yes.

(*A* WAITRESS *comes with a tray of glasses.*)

CUDDEFORD: Champagne?

HOME SECRETARY: Thank you.

CUDDEFORD: Please. Leave the fishy stuff there.

(*The* HOME SECRETARY *takes a glass of champagne. The* WAITRESS *puts a pot of caviare down next to them on a small table.*)

HOME SECRETARY: Yes, it's good to have a context for any important policy debate.

CUDDEFORD: Yes, that's right. (*He smiles.*) Believe me, the judges understand, in all questions dealing with the future of the bar, the government must act. It must do whatever it thinks best. But always within the framework of the constitution.

HOME SECRETARY: Yes. (*He looks at him a moment, wary.*) Well, surely.

CUDDEFORD: But you hardly need me to remind you of that.

HOME SECRETARY: No.

(*The* TOASTMASTER *has already announced the latest arrival.*)

TOASTMASTER: Sir Peter Edgecombe QC.

(*They turn at once to greet* SIR PETER, *immaculate in white tie.*)

HOME SECRETARY: Good Lord, look who's here.

CUDDEFORD: Do you know Sir Peter?

HOME SECRETARY: Do I know Sir Peter?

(*He repeats the question as if it were ridiculous. They shake hands warmly.*)

SIR PETER: Welcome, Kevin. So, how are you?

HOME SECRETARY: I was talking only yesterday to the Prime Minister. You'll be pleased to hear your name came up.

SIR PETER: Oh, really? (*He smiles, involuntarily.*) How interesting.

CUDDEFORD: That's good for you, Peter.

SIR PETER: Yes.

HOME SECRETARY: We actually discussed you for quite a long time.

SIR PETER: I'm very flattered.

HOME SECRETARY: We couldn't work it out. We were both wondering why on earth you took the Piaf.

(CUDDEFORD *smiles, delighted.* SIR PETER *looks miffed.*)

CUDDEFORD: Yes, that question has puzzled some of us here.

SIR PETER: I don't really think it should monopolize our conversation. When there are so many more important issues in the air.

HOME SECRETARY: Goodness. Are there?

(*He says this mildly, smiling, then, in order to divert the conversation, picks up a menu card from the table.*)

'Roast Venison Baden-Baden.' Just exactly how is that done?

(CUDDEFORD *smiles.*)

CUDDEFORD: I think you'll find it's a young roebuck.

HOME SECRETARY: Ah yes.

CUDDEFORD: It's been shot through the heart and then skinned. Then basted in some sort of fruity, substantial gravy.

HOME SECRETARY: Good gracious.

CUDDEFORD: Then it's served up to us.

(*He smiles. The* HOME SECRETARY *watches him, a little*

bemused, but too old a hand to let himself show it.)
As you know, we have a system whereby law students have to eat dinners to qualify.

HOME SECRETARY: I've heard that.

CUDDEFORD: They have to eat twenty-four dinners each. We were proposing to abolish this requirement as outdated. But then we found that without this, so to speak, ready-made pool of captive consumers, the entire kitchen effort would not be economic.

HOME SECRETARY: That's tricky.

CUDDEFORD: Hence we would not be able to give ourselves lunch.

(*The* HOME SECRETARY *looks at* SIR PETER.)

SIR PETER: It's true.

CUDDEFORD: And that of course would be catastrophic.

HOME SECRETARY: I see that.

CUDDEFORD: The law is a college. We meet. We talk. A judge perhaps has a word with a barrister. He says nothing overt. Nothing critical. Maybe only a look, a chance remark. And yet all the time . . . there are hints. Thanks to these a barrister is learning. The social *is* the professional. (*He smiles.*) How do you put a true price on that?

HOME SECRETARY: Well, it's hard . . .

CUDDEFORD: It's not quantifiable.

HOME SECRETARY: No.

(CUDDEFORD *looks him in the eye.*)

CUDDEFORD: It adds to a richness of culture, a depth, a breadth of vision you only find in an Inn.

(*The* HOME SECRETARY *again looks across to* SIR PETER.)

SIR PETER: He's right.

CUDDEFORD: For instance, tonight, when the loyal toast is proposed, we do not rise. Did you know this?

HOME SECRETARY: Why, no.

CUDDEFORD: By special dispensation. From Charles the Second, no less. At a dinner here, he gave permission, in perpetuity, that this would be the only place in the kingdom where people do not rise to say God Save the King.

HOME SECRETARY: I'm astonished.

CUDDEFORD: He did it because he himself was too drunk to stand up. (*He nods, suddenly incisive.*) Now it's *this*, it's this sort of thing, Home Secretary . . .

HOME SECRETARY: Kevin . . .

CUDDEFORD: What would you call it? This slow *silting* of tradition, this centuries-long building-up, this accumulation of strata, which makes the great rock on which we now do things. It's infinitely precious.

(*The* HOME SECRETARY *frowns.*)

HOME SECRETARY: Yes, but it must also be open to change.

CUDDEFORD: *Open.*

(*He says it enthusiastically.*)

HOME SECRETARY: It must not become hidebound.

CUDDEFORD: Hidebound?

HOME SECRETARY: Yes.

CUDDEFORD: Small chance of that! (*He leans forward, sure of himself.*) Remember, all the time judging brings you in touch with ordinary people. In our courts. We see them every day. Ordinary, common-as-muck individuals. Some of them quite ghastly, I promise you that. (*He nods.*) This makes us alert to public opinion. We're closer to it, perhaps, than you think.

HOME SECRETARY: Are you?

CUDDEFORD: It's reflected in the way we sentence. Everyone claims it's our fault if we sentence too high. But the tariff for rape . . .

HOME SECRETARY: I know . . .

CUDDEFORD: . . . has shot up from what?

HOME SECRETARY: I know this . . .

CUDDEFORD: . . . Maybe eighteen months deferred to over five years. It's not at *our* wish. It's because we have listened to what the public, at least the female part of it, wants us to do. (*The* HOME SECRETARY *is smiling, familiar with this argument.*)

HOME SECRETARY: Yes, I admit. But it's a rare exception. There are figures from Germany. Did you read those?

(CUDDEFORD *frowns.*)

CUDDEFORD: Germany? No.

HOME SECRETARY: I sent them over. I circulated all High Court judges.

52

CUDDEFORD: I read little from Germany.
  (*He turns to* SIR PETER, *diverting, but the* HOME SECRETARY
  is not letting him off the hook.)
  Like most judges, I have no time to read, off the case.
  Maybe, if I'm lucky, a thriller . . .
HOME SECRETARY: There they've reduced all prison sentences
  radically, by up to one-quarter, even one-third, without any
  effect on the criminal statistics.
  (CUDDEFORD *looks at him warily.*)
CUDDEFORD: Really? Germany?
HOME SECRETARY: The same is true in Sweden.
CUDDEFORD: Sweden? (*He turns to* SIR PETER.) Peter, had you
  heard this?
SIR PETER: No. No, actually. (*He looks down, feeling himself on
  thin ice.*) Word hadn't reached me.
CUDDEFORD: It hadn't reached me either. (*He frowns.*) I think it's
  to do with the mail.
  (*The* HOME SECRETARY *looks at him a little more severely, as if
  finally showing a little steel.*)
HOME SECRETARY: Yes, it's a fact, it's true, government is
  nervous of bullying. As you pointed out, the constitutional
  proprieties must be observed.
CUDDEFORD: Indeed.
HOME SECRETARY: Yes, they must. But, to be frank, we're
  reaching a point where we'll run out of ways of requesting
  the judiciary to be less *trigger-happy*.
  (CUDDEFORD *looks at him a moment, noting the last word.*)
  I know of course it's none of my business . . .
CUDDEFORD: Well . . .
HOME SECRETARY: I'm only the Home Secretary, I wouldn't
  dream of interfering . . .
CUDDEFORD: No.
HOME SECRETARY: I know how wrong that would be.
  Constitutionally.
CUDDEFORD: It would.
HOME SECRETARY: An independent judiciary is perhaps the most
  important bullwark against chaos this country has. (*He looks
  CUDDEFORD *in the eye.*) But we've nowhere to put all these
  bloody prisoners you keep sending us. (*He checks himself,*

impeccably polite.) And that is something you must take on board.

(CUDDEFORD *just looks at him*.)

CUDDEFORD: Yes.

HOME SECRETARY: Why can't you see that?

CUDDEFORD: We do. (*He moves towards him, smiling, quiet now*.) We do, Home Secretary. But truly it is your problem, not ours.

(*Before the* HOME SECRETARY *can respond, he goes on*.) You see, just think, if for one single moment, when I'm at work in my court, if I begin to consider . . . if I ever consider what prison is now like . . . then I cannot fairly administer justice. Because my head is full of what we may call the failings of society . . . (*He shakes his head regretfully*.) Which are truly not my concern. (*He looks at the* HOME SECRETARY.) It's actually dangerous. If I and my colleagues begin to deceive ourselves, if we fudge our principles, if when the accused stands before us, some extraneous factor, however pressing, makes us pretend that crime is not crime, and should not be punished, then the judges become an instrument of government convenience. (*He smiles*.) And, as you said earlier, that is not what you want.

(*The* HOME SECRETARY *looks at him warily*.)

HOME SECRETARY: No.

CUDDEFORD: Believe me, I know, I do understand you. Tonight in your cells, I appreciate you have twice as many prisoners as places. It's sad. It's regrettable. These poor devils, they prey on my mind.

HOME SECRETARY: Then why don't you act?

(CUDDEFORD *looks at him and smiles, not taking the question seriously, but turning good-humouredly to* SIR PETER.)

CUDDEFORD: Haven't I explained? Haven't I just said to you? (*He leans in, taking the* HOME SECRETARY'S *arm*.) And mightn't I ask the same thing of you?

(*Before he can say more, the* TOASTMASTER *interrupts*.)

TOASTMASTER: My Lords, Ladies and Gentlemen, dinner is served.

(CUDDEFORD *pats the* HOME SECRETARY'S *arm good-humouredly, before heading off to find the high commissioner*.)

CUDDEFORD: And now we've talked enough shop. Where's the high commissioner? Take your places, please everyone, before we go in.

(*The* HOME SECRETARY *puts his glass down as everyone teams up with a partner and gets into an orderly line of twos, before going in.* SIR PETER *hovers, waiting for the* HOME SECRETARY.)

HOME SECRETARY: What do you say, Sir Peter?

SIR PETER: I say there's one thing to be grateful for.

HOME SECRETARY: Oh yes? And what's that?

SIR PETER: The British police.

(*The* HOME SECRETARY *frowns.*)

HOME SECRETARY: I'm not sure I know what you mean.

SIR PETER: It is one of the great mercies of your situation that only 3 per cent of all crimes reach the courts. (*He smiles.*) Just imagine the scale of your problems if the police began to have some significant success.

HOME SECRETARY: Yes, I must say.

SIR PETER: The system is already strained to breaking point by a force which is catching scarcely anyone at all.

(*They find themselves the pair at the end of the line.* SIR PETER *reaches for his arm to draw him in to the crocodile.*)

Kevin, you do have that to be grateful for.

(CUDDEFORD *is standing next to the high commissioner at the head of the line.* SIR PETER *and the* HOME SECRETARY *are at the back.*)

CUDDEFORD: Gentlemen, the bell is about to be rung.

(*The stage is suddenly still and the whole Hall falls quiet. A bell sounds. The lights go out and the group stands a moment in the darkness, the lights of the candles burning far from them. They set off in orderly crocodile and make their way in silence to the table. When they get there each goes to his place.* CUDDEFORD *is standing at the centre.*)

The eyes of all things look up and put their trust in Thee, O Lord. Thou Givest them their Meat in Due Season, Thou Openest Thine Hands and fillest with Thy blessing every living Thing. Replenish our Hearts with Joy and Gladness that We, having sufficient, may be Rich and Plentiful in good works. God Save Thy Church, the Queen, the Royal

Family and this Realm; God Send us Peace and Truth in
Christ Our Lord.

ALL: Amen.

(*There is a second only, but before they can even sit down the
dinner fades from view.*)

SCENE THREE

*Night in the charge room. The area is only half-lit, so we see an image
more like a Victorian schoolroom than a police station – groups of
coppers working on their papers, their tongues in their cheeks, fingers
inky, like children sitting for exams. The boisterousness of the day is
suspended. At the front* JIMMY *arrives to address us, some sheets of
paper in his hand.*

JIMMY: Already, you know, you can see the ones you fancy. It
gets to be obvious after a while. I can throw my eyes down a
crime sheet already, and pick the ones where I'll get a result.
(*He holds up the list to show the audience.*) There's maybe
thirty-five cases. Most of them you haven't got a chance.
Like burglaries, muggings, forget it, unless someone caught
them red-handed. Which if they did, it sure wasn't us. An
officer on the beat witnesses – actually witnesses – one crime
in ten years. Then maybe the case you choose isn't moving
very quickly. What happens? Some pen-pusher comes down
from upstairs, says, look, the press are on to us, we need a
nice graph. Now the problem with graphs is, visually
speaking, people prefer it when they go up. (*He relaxes,
enjoying himself.*) So you go down a club, you pull in seven
kids, it's not very hard. You do them for possession, let them
off with a caution, and everything's fine. Seven crimes, seven
clear-ups. Oh yes, they all count. And everyone's happy with
cautions. None of that senseless ferrying, none of those
expensive appearances in court. It's public relations. We
know that. So does everyone. Except for the public, of
course. But public relations is always a bit of a toupee. If you
can tell what it is, then it's not any good.

(*At once a* YOUNG POLICEMAN *and* POLICEWOMAN *appear,*

56

struggling with two immigrants, one MAN, *one* WOMAN. *The*
MAN *is protesting at being held, while the* WOMAN *is keeping up*
an unceasing line of complaint about her rights. As they come
through the charge-room door, making a racket, JIMMY *goes*
back to consult the charge-room book.)

MAN: *Choldo! Mey keyta hun mujhey choldo!*

WOMAN: *Tumara haq nahi hai. Tum yey nahi kurr suktey. Yey*
kanoon kay khelaf hai. Mujhey vakil sey millney kar haq hai.

MAN: *Mujhey haat mutt legow.*

YOUNG POLICEMAN: Come on, now, come on, stop pissing me
about now! (*He suddenly loses his temper.*) Stop pissing me
about!
(*And he begins to get pretty rough as he bundles the* MAN *towards*
the cells.)

WOMAN: *Humarey dost Heathrow pay hai, Humarey sarey jaaney*
walley Heathrow pay hai. Yey humara haq hai. Tumara koi haq
nahi bunta yey kurr ney keyliey.

MAN: *Choldo! Choldo!*
(LESTER *has now come in and shouts at* TOBY *to get him to go*
and help.)

LESTER: Toby, go and deal with those bastards . . .

TOBY: All right, all right . . .

LESTER: Go and deal with them. Give Micky a hand with that lot.
I don't care what you do to them. I can't bloody stand it. I've
bloody had it for today.

TOBY: I'm going, don't worry.
(*From the other direction comes* ESTHER *in her police shirt, a*
very tight skirt and black stockings, a pile of documents under her
arm.)

ESTHER: Come on, now, Lester, don't lose your rag.
(JIMMY, *his work obviously disturbed, appears from the CID*
room. He is in his shirt-sleeves, but manages to look as elegant as
usual.)

JIMMY: What on earth's happening?

LESTER: Immigration cases. We're holding them for Hounslow.
I've already rung Hounslow five times.

ESTHER: Of course you have, darling.
(JIMMY *just smiles at* ESTHER *as* LESTER *gathers up the things*
he needs.)

57

LESTER: I hate immigration. Domestics. Drunks.

(ESTHER *puts her papers down right next to him, and bumps her hip into him in a comradely way.*)

And bloody women.

ESTHER: Yeah. I've heard you hate us as well.

(*The noise from the cells is beginning to abate. The shouting has finished but the banging goes on.*)

JIMMY: It's his mother's fault.

ESTHER: You're kidding. What did she do to you?

LESTER: She didn't do anything. She just told me one day you all had an extra pair of teeth. (*He smiles at her quickly, looking up from the desk.*) I'm not saying where.

JIMMY: What he means is, he's never found them.

LESTER: No, but I've had fun looking.

JIMMY: Esther'll show you hers if you like.

(LESTER *is now on his way out, at speed.* ESTHER *flashes a smile at* JIMMY.)

ESTHER: Yeah. I've had mine capped. And sharpened.

(LESTER *jumps a little way into the air and shudders.*)

LESTER: Oh God, I can't wait.

(*As he goes out, he passes* DAVE LAWRENCE, *who is coming back from the direction of the cells with a black man in his thirties, very large but very gentle, a big soft man who is wearing khaki trousers and an American jacket. His name is* JASON SMITH *and he is very distressed.* DAVE *is carrying a print-out which he takes straight to the duty desk.* JIMMY *has wandered round and is now standing checking the day's crime list.*)

JASON: Don't do this to me, I beg of you. Look, I beg of you, I was just at a party, all right?

JIMMY: OK, Dave?

(DAVE *gives a nod of recognition.* JASON *is carrying some photos which he now holds up.*)

JASON: It's my mate. Look at this. All right? He's sitting on a tank. Tomorrow he's going to the desert. He's going to the desert. Imagine that. Be fair. Just imagine it.

(DAVE *has calmly got out a form and is taking little notice.*)

DAVE: I think I can imagine it. Look, put away the happy snaps.

JASON: You don't know my wife. She'll kill me. I promise you, she'll kill me when she finds out.

58

(ESTHER *looks at him, a quick glance, then away, as* JASON *persists.*)

Why me? Why did you choose me?

DAVE: We didn't choose you.

JASON: You did. There's thousands out there.

DAVE: You went through a red light.

JASON: It wasn't red. It was orange.

DAVE: Well, it doesn't matter.

JASON: So I lose my licence. Are you saying that's it?

DAVE: It's an automatic penalty. You're 70 over. For a 70 reading it's automatic. (*He looks up a moment.*) I'm sorry, mate. There's nothing I can do.

(LESTER *returns, still frazzled, walking heavily back to his place. The noise from the cells has stopped.* JIMMY *has taken over the crime book and gone to look it over in the corner.* ESTHER, *standing, is writing on top of the filing cabinet.* JASON *moves now to the centre of the room to address everyone. They ignore him.*)

JASON: I don't get it. I don't bloody get it. I'm always there for you. I'm a bloody builder. A builder, all right? Can't you tell the difference? (*He suddenly turns, furious.*) What's the point? What's the point of trying? Why bother to be normal? If you go through with this, I tell you what I'll do. I'm going to get a bobble hat and grow bloody dreadlocks. Because if this is what happens, I might as well.

(*There is silence in the room. Everyone carries on working.*)

Why do you choose us? The law-abiding people? There's so much scum on the street. Why not pick up the scum? I'm always there for you. I see an accident, it's me that gets out, says, 'Can I help you, officer?' I help you. I always help. Why pick on me? I'm not a pusher. I'm not a pimp. (*He shakes his head.*) You want to know how to piss off law-abiding citizens?

DAVE: Thank you, we're pretty good at it already, to be honest, we don't need any tips.

JASON: Do you know this saying? We've got a saying. Have you heard this? We call people 'rubber heels'.

(DAVE *looks at him mistrustfully.*)

DAVE: No.

59

JASON: We use it. We use it for people who creep up behind you and bugger their own.

(*At this last remark of Jason's,* LESTER *suddenly blows his top, throwing his chair back as he gets up, and homing in on* JASON *with real power.*)

LESTER: All right, that's enough of this, I've heard enough of this.

(*A couple of people look up at Lester's explosion, but nobody says anything.*)

At a 70 reading you can actually kill people. You can kill with a car. If you drive at 70, you're a major liability. You can kill yourself at the same time.

(JASON *is looking at him, stunned.*)

All right, I shan't pretend that really matters. Why should it? You've acted like a prick.

JASON: I know.

(*He pauses, the wind suddenly gone out of him. The two big men are standing directly opposite each other in the middle of the room, and now Jason's manner, in a drinker's switch, changes from angry to pathetic.*)

I know I have.

LESTER: But I'm only interested in protecting the public. Who may get killed by people like you.

(JASON *nods, contrite.*)

JASON: I want to say sorry.

LESTER: All right.

JASON: OK.

(LESTER *stands a moment, hands on hips, letting* JASON *calm down.*)

I'm going down on my knees.

(JASON *suddenly kneels in front of* LESTER *in the middle of the room. There is a sudden, uneasy silence throughout the room.*)

ESTHER: Anyone want tea?

JASON: I'm on my knees to you, skip. My wife and I, we're going through changes. Think. I'm a builder. I lose my licence, I tell you, I'm nothing. Without a licence, I'm nothing. I'm a Paddy in the Falls Road. I can't pay the bills, skip. I lose my licence, and what can I do?

(*There is a long silence.* LESTER *stands, uncomfortable.* JIMMY *doesn't look up.*)

JIMMY: I hate it when they grovel.

(DAVE *is quite still, just watching.*)

DAVE: You better get up, mate. I don't have that power. Nor does
he. It's not up to us. It's a process, all right?

(SANDRA *comes in, in shirtsleeves, and sees the kneeling man at
Lester's feet.*)

SANDRA: Hello, what's this? A proposal of marriage?

(LESTER *moves away, back to his seat.* DAVE *moves over to help
JASON up.*)

DAVE: Come on, old mate.

SANDRA: Gosh, Lester. You're marrying a client. When's the
happy day?

(LESTER *scowls at her.*)

Good evening, Jimmy.

JIMMY: Hello, Sandra.

(*She opens a drawer beside* LESTER.)

LESTER: What are you after?

SANDRA: The key to the property cupboard.

LESTER: What's going on?

SANDRA: Nothing. I was just looking. Oh, for something from an
old job. An old case.

(*She smiles casually at* JIMMY *and moves away as* ESTHER *turns
with a glossy document in her hand. She holds it up.*)

ESTHER: I'm meant to be organizing the divisional skiing party.
Anyone fancy it?

SANDRA: No, thanks, Esther.

(SANDRA *goes to a desk at the side of the room, where she sits to
write out notes from her notebook.* JASON *is being led out,
shaking his head, by* DAVE.)

JASON: I wouldn't do this to you.

DAVE: And then we're going to charge you formally. And then
we'll put you in a taxi, all right?

(*They go.* ESTHER *is beside* LESTER *with the glossy brochure.*)

ESTHER: Fun on the slopes, yes, Lester?

LESTER: No, thank you, honestly. I don't think my marriage
would last.

(JIMMY *chuckles.*)

JIMMY: Can he bring his wife, that's what Lester's asking.

LESTER: Don't even mention her. Do you know she's found a
new word?

ESTHER: What's that?

LESTER: I think she sits reading dictionaries. I got in from the relief at seven thirty this morning, she was still in bed, I got in, she said, 'You know what our relationship needs?' (ESTHER *smiles*.)

ESTHER: I can't think.

LESTER: 'What I'd like', she said, 'is less sex and more cherishing.' (*He shakes his head and looks round the room.*) Cherishing! Does anyone know what that means? (*He smiles across at* JIMMY.) You done any cherishing, Jimmy?

JIMMY: Not that I can recall.

ESTHER: You can cherish on the slopes. That's what we go for. We'll be cherishing. You can cherish all night if you like. Well, at least, cherishing and drinking.

LESTER: Oh well, in that case, I might come along.

(*The both smile.* ESTHER *moves away, as* BARRY *comes in, in shirtsleeves, carrying the usual polystyrene cup of coffee, a file and various metal objects in evidence bags.*)

BARRY: Abstracting electricity! Is that the most boring crime of all time?

(JIMMY *looks up. But* SANDRA, *working at the back, doesn't turn.*)

JIMMY: Barry.

ESTHER: I don't know what it is.

LESTER: Fiddling the meter.

ESTHER: Oh, I see.

BARRY: In this case, at a squat! At a squat! For about fifteen quid. I mean, can you think of anything more pointless?

LESTER: What, than them doing it? Or us pursuing it?

BARRY: Both. Who gives a damn? (*He tosses the evidence bags down on the desk and sits down addressing the whole room.*) I mean, do you give a damn? (*He shakes his head.*) I read this statistic. If you take all the crime, all of it, every single bit, in money it doesn't amount every year to what's lost in tax evasion. (*He gestures round the huge room.*) And yet, look at us! Here we all are.

LESTER: Sure.

BARRY: What is it? One hundred and thirty thousand policemen. Twenty-eight thousand in London alone. To collect a sum of

62

money – at incredible expense – which is actually less than the government happily lets rich bastards get up and walk away with every year. (*He shakes his head.*) I mean, please tell me, what is the point?

(LESTER *smiles and gets up.*)

LESTER: I can't answer that, Barry.

BARRY: Come on, I'm asking you.

LESTER: It's too deep for me. (*On the way out, he puts a friendly hand on Barry's shoulder.*) You should go on *Mastermind*. Come on, Esther, we're charging this geezer.

ESTHER: I'm coming. I'm on my way.

(ESTHER *follows* LESTER *out.* JIMMY *has got up and is sorting through the things* BARRY *has thrown down.* SANDRA *has still not turned round.*)

JIMMY: You didn't see Dubin?

BARRY: I certainly didn't.

JIMMY: The boss is after us. Guess why.

(BARRY *smiles.*)

Too much overtime.

BARRY: Oh, you don't say.

JIMMY: He says we're way over budget. He says we've been coming on at five for surveillance without waking him up and asking him first.

(JIMMY *is gathering his stuff up now, smiling.*)

BARRY: So what's he going to do? Impound my BMW?

JIMMY: He says he knows exactly how you got that new set of steel wheels.

BARRY: Well, he's *right*. By catching thieves. That's how I got them. By getting up at five and doing the job.

(*He has a sort of generalized ill humour, but* JIMMY *has heard it before.*)

JIMMY: Yeah, OK . . .

BARRY: But of course that's way out of fashion. We should all sit in the nick and make policy drafts. It's what we all say. It's all public relations.

JIMMY: Sure. It doesn't bother me. Because *I'm* public relations. I'd have to be stupid not to know that. (*He heads out of the room.*) When your name is Abdul, and they all call you Jimmy, it does give you a certain perspective on things.

63

(*And* JIMMY'*s gone.* BARRY *just smiles, agreeing with him, almost not noticing that he and* SANDRA *are now alone.*)

BARRY: Yeah, we're all part of it. Define your objectives, fulfil your flow chart, manage your resources, keep your paper straight.

(*He turns, finding himself abandoned in the huge room.* SANDRA *is still facing away.*)

Hello. How are you?

SANDRA: Fine.

BARRY: I haven't seen you.

SANDRA: No. (*And now for the first time she turns and looks at him. She is very quiet.*) I wonder why not.

(BARRY *frowns.*)

I waited for you.

BARRY: Did you?

SANDRA: Yes. At the usual place.

BARRY: Oh, shit, really? I had a rugby match. I meant to say. (*He looks at her briefly, then away.*) Sometimes I do get tired of the secrecy. It makes the whole thing seem silly. Assignations. Times and places.

SANDRA: Yes.

(*They both smile.*)

But perhaps you should have called me. Perhaps if you'd called me, I wouldn't have felt effed and left.

(BARRY *waits a moment, not wanting to rise to this.*)

BARRY: No.

SANDRA: Besides, I always thought you rather liked secrecy. I thought you got a buzz from it. Not looking at each other when we're at work. All that. Having one over them. Don't you rather like that? Isn't having secrets your favourite thing? (*She smiles.*) What changed your mind?

BARRY: Nothing's changed.

SANDRA: Hasn't it?

BARRY: No. (*He waits a moment, uncomfortable.*) Why don't we talk about it next week? When we're on day relief? It's easier. I think I'm too tired.

SANDRA: What, and you've got a headache as well?

(*He smiles, trying to keep it light.*)

BARRY: Come on, Sandra, this isn't like you.

SANDRA: I'm always so easy, is that what you mean?

BARRY: I didn't have you down as a nagger.

SANDRA: Thanks, Barry. (*She looks at him, and then speaks in a more dangerous tone.*) But ask the boys, they'll tell you . . . all women are.

(*He catches her tone, and turns to look at her, finally giving way, to explain himself.*)

BARRY: I'm sorry. It's just a bad time. You know, we all have them. You try to keep cheerful. It's part of the job. (*He smiles.*) I used to think at the end of my marriage, you know, in the last days with Kay, if you're a copper, it's a bit pointless trying. You come home. 'Oh, can you wash my shirt, darling? It's got gob all over it. Yeah, I got spat on in the street. No, it didn't bother me. I'll just go upstairs and read to the kid.'

(*He looks down, thoughtful now.* SANDRA *just watches, not reacting.*)

All that stuff makes you cautious.

SANDRA: I know that.

BARRY: The job does.

SANDRA: I know.

(*There's a pause.*)

What are you saying? That I get too close?

BARRY: No. Not you. No. Never. (*He turns and looks at her.*) Never you, Sandra.

(*She waits a moment.*)

SANDRA: Then, what?

(*She waits for him to go on, but he says nothing more.*)

I think this is to do with McKinnon. And Travis. And Faulkner.

BARRY: Do you?

SANDRA: Yes.

(*It is suddenly completely quiet in the station, the two of them tense now across the room.*)

BARRY: What makes you say that?

SANDRA: Because something happened. I talked to you that day when we were in here. Then, next day – wham – the iron curtain came down. (*She is very quiet.*) You forget. I know you, Barry. It's very insulting. I'm on your side. Don't you know that?

(*He is just looking at her, thoughtfully, giving nothing away.*)
What happened in the flat?

BARRY: Nothing. Nothing. Really. I promise you.

SANDRA: It's me. (*She waits.*) It's me, Barry.

BARRY: So? It was our operation. It's over. What's the interest?
It's personal. It's my method. It's private.
(*He looks at her to close the subject.*)

SANDRA: And have you heard McKinnon is going to appeal?
(BARRY *smiles, relieved at the change of subject, and at once able to relax.*)

BARRY: Oh sure, yeah . . .

SANDRA: What do you think?

BARRY: I think, why shouldn't he? He'll try and get his sentence
cut. Fair enough. He's learnt pretty fast. He'll play the
system. He'll have his go. That's the game.

SANDRA: Do you think he's got a chance?

BARRY: Why are you asking me? It's not in my hands. (*He smiles,
then is suddenly firm, as if his patience were worn down.*) Yes, I
mean *no*, since you ask me. To be honest, he shouldn't be in
prison. But then none of them should. Because it isn't a
deterrent. He shouldn't be in prison because prison doesn't
work. I'd dye them. No, really. I mean it. The colour
according to what they're found to have done. Give them red
hands for a burglary. If it's a sex offence, paint their heads
green. There should be a code, so we all know. So we can all
laugh at them. (*He shakes his head.*) I'm serious, Sandra.

SANDRA: I know you are. (*She looks at him a moment.*) There was
this woman once. I was on traffic duty. I'd had twenty-ton
lorries pushing smoke up my nostrils all day. She was half
into a bus lane. I was pretty foul to her, nothing excessive, I
was cutting, I was just short. You know what she said?
'Jesus, you've all got so touchy. Talking to the police is now
like dealing with an ethnic minority.'
(BARRY *turns away, really irritated by this story.*)

BARRY: Oh sure, hell, what does she know?

SANDRA: You've got to fight it, Barry.

BARRY: Don't tell *me* to fight it.

SANDRA: You're getting ratty as hell. You're getting like the
others. You know that.

BARRY: Oh, and you aren't? (*He turns away, furious, but laughing at her now.*) Oh, of course not, you're on the way *up*, I forgot. You're doing the *exams*. You'll get a Toblerone to put on your desk with your name on it, you'll get the braid, the only problem is . . . (*He stops a moment, smiling, sure of his point.*) Did anyone mention this? What comes with promotion? Did anyone *say*?

SANDRA: What?

(*He just smiles, infuriating.*)

What?

BARRY: Did anyone come up to you? Did they say, 'Oh, by the way, there is one drawback. It comes with the car and the pension. You have to buy into the bullshit as well.'

SANDRA: Oh, really?

BARRY: Yeah. (*He moves a little towards her, quietly triumphant.*) If you stay where I am, if you stick in the ranks, if you're a grunt in the canteen, well, we may be low, but we do have one big advantage. (*He smiles.*) We don't have to pretend that everything's great.

(*They are standing opposite each other now, still separated in the big room.* SANDRA *is holding down her anger.*)

SANDRA: Well, of course I don't have your experience. No one beats you for that, Barry. You're our man on the street. Everyone's favourite policeman. Totally competent. And totally defensive. (*She stops suddenly, a change in her tone.*) I've been trying to find out just why that is.

(BARRY *marks the change, watching her dispassionately.*)

BARRY: What does that mean?

SANDRA: I took out the file. Yeah. On the Faulkner case. I read the report from the lab.

BARRY: Why? (*He is calm, not raising his voice.*) Why did you do that?

SANDRA: I've also just looked in the property cupboard. You ought to be more careful, you know.

(*He stands, giving nothing away.*)

The aspirin's just sitting there. Why didn't you get rid of it?

BARRY: Because nobody's interested.

(*He looks at her, as if trying to work out how to handle this.*)

At least no one was until now. Hello, Toby.

(TOBY *has stuck his head round the charge-room door.*)

TOBY: You haven't seen Lester?

(BARRY *walks casually away from* SANDRA *and goes to sit down, at his ease.*)

SANDRA: Yeah, he's in with the immigrants.

TOBY: I've got to go and get a bail-jumper.

(BARRY *laughs and looks at his watch.*)

BARRY: Spare us, Toby. It's one o'clock.

TOBY: We never close.

BARRY: Well, he's out there.

TOBY: Thanks. I'll get my body. I'll be back in a mo.

(*He goes out the main charge-room door to the outside.* BARRY *has picked up his cup and is smiling.* SANDRA *is reasonable, gentle.*)

SANDRA: I'm not threatening you, Barry. Why would I want to? (*She smiles.*) It's just if you look at it . . . I mean only for a moment . . . if you were to look at it from my point of view. It's true, I'm a high-flyer, as everyone keeps telling me, they've chosen me, I'm going up. But that shouldn't mean being taken for an idiot. That feeling's not good. I tell you, you wouldn't like it. Does going up mean that you turn a blind eye? (*She shakes her head.*) Because if that's it, it's buying into a nightmare. It makes everything a lie. Yeah, go up, head on up. But turn your face away from what's going on below you. Turn into a spaghetti-head. Meaning: just keep out of it. Pretend nothing's happening. (*She looks down.*) I'm sorry. But I want to find out.

(*He looks at her a moment, thoughtfully.*)

BARRY: When I was little, I used to go to the pictures. Every week there was always this guy. He was the hero. Why was he the hero? Because he was the one who said no . . . (*He looks up to check she recognizes this.*) He had this kind of certainty. Something was going on. Always. Every week. And every week this bloke'd get up, there was usually some sort of meeting, he'd say, 'Now look here, I think this is wrong . . .' And the others would all look kind of puzzled and hostile, and he'd say, 'I don't care, I don't care what you think. OK, I'm out on my own. But there's something more important than any of us . . . yes, you see, there's a *principle*

68

here . . .' (*He smiles.*) And I used to think, now why exactly
am I meant to like this geezer? I know I'm meant to say,
'Wow, what a guy.' But I don't. (*He turns now and looks at*
SANDRA, *sure of his point.*) And you don't actually, Sandra,
all your instincts are exactly like mine . . .
(*She shifts, uneasy.*)
SANDRA: I'm not sure what you mean.
BARRY: I mean, I didn't like him. That stuff is so easy. 'Me and
my conscience.' That's the easy route. The hard route's the
other one, the one that's taken by all the poor bloody foot-
soldiers, like Lester and Jimmy and Dave . . . (*He gestures
offstage.*) Who'd never even think of betraying their pals. But
they have a talent which no one else has. Their talent is for
turning up every day. (*He nods.*) Yeah. For being there.
And, OK, there's a lot of moaning, they moan in the
canteen, they whinge, they complain about the job. But they
keep on doing it. And all the shit is landed in their laps. And
nobody thanks them. On the contrary, it's all directives, it's
supervision, it's behavioural correction courses, it's 'Did I
hear you make a sexist remark?' (*He gets up, acting out the
questions.*) It's 'Are you racist? Are you foul-mouthed? Do
you never lose your temper? Do you censor your speech?'
(*He nods.*) Do you put up with all this, all day, day in, day
out? Being treated on sufferance? Being scapegoats for
everything that goes wrong? 'Oh, there's a traffic jam.
There's a drug epidemic. Crime's on the increase. The young
have no respect any more. We're not free to demonstrate.
We're not allowed to strike.' (*He stops.*) *'I didn't win the pools
last week.'* (*He turns savagely towards her.*) 'Hey, wait a
moment, tell you what . . . *Let's blame the police . . .*'
(*But* SANDRA *is not giving way.*)
SANDRA: What are you saying? That we're all beyond criticism?
BARRY: No. No, I'm not saying that, I'm saying, you stand there,
Sandra, you tell stories about how we're all getting touchy.
Touchy? Really? You're *touchy*? When people say
everything's your fault? I can't think why. Surely you can
take twenty-four-hour round-the-clock criticism, and learn
not to react? (*He stops, suddenly quietening to make his point.*)
Well, actually you can. By dissembling. That's how you do

it. By being secret. By doing things your way. (*He smiles.*) Yes, a copper is allowed something. It's all he's got. You're allowed a few private moments with criminals. You're allowed a way of doing things which is actually your own. (*Sandra's gaze does not waver. She is quiet when she speaks, not accusing.*)

SANDRA: You mean you're bent?

(*There is a silence.* BARRY *is so angry at the question that his reply comes out as politeness, ice cold.*)

BARRY: I'm sorry?

SANDRA: You mean those men are innocent?

(*Again he pauses, to repress his anger.*)

BARRY: No. No, they're not. Remember, we found the stolen goods.

SANDRA: If they're guilty, then why are you so defensive?

BARRY: The obvious reason. I don't think I've done anything wrong. (*He looks at her a moment.*) I'll tell you what I did. I went in there, all right? I knew this gang of old. I thought, this is it. This is what you wait for. So . . . yes . . . I came up with the bag. (*He nods.*) Of course it was aspirin. That was the bluff. But they have to believe you're mad enough. That's what's important. (*He smiles.*) You've never seen it but I've got a good act.

SANDRA: Yes, I'm sure.

BARRY: I had to convince them. They had to believe it could be cocaine.

SANDRA: And did they?

BARRY: Why, yes. I said, 'I'm going to send this stuff to the lab. If it comes back labelled what I think it is, then you're both down for an extra five years. You're looking at a total of twelve or thirteen. How do you like that? Just think of it. Well, you've got it. Unless . . .'

(*He stops.*)

SANDRA: Unless what?

(*He turns away, frustrated.*)

BARRY: Sandra, what's *power*? What's power for a policeman?

SANDRA: I don't know. Tell me.

BARRY: 'Unless . . .' (*He suspends the sentence a moment.*) 'You give me information.'

SANDRA: And they did?

BARRY: Why, sure. Yes, surely. For God's sake, Sandra, that's all you need. (*He laughs with excitement at it.*) So, yes, three weeks later in the City of London, when some bullion robbers – Kilmartin? Remember? Yes, you've heard the name, it was all over the papers – when Kilmartin and his lot turned up on the job, thanks to that little bag I waved at Travis and Faulkner, the Flying Squad was waiting. Bang! Double bubble! *Two* lots of villains. No sweat. Both gangs very nasty, all very nasty people. More or less perfect. (*He nods, pleased with this.*) And what's more I'm up for the Commissioner's medal.

(*But before he has even said this, SANDRA has moved away slowly across the room, thinking it all out.*)

SANDRA: Barry, you're out of your mind.

BARRY: I'm out of my mind?

SANDRA: Yes.

BARRY: Kilmartin's gang had shotguns.

SANDRA: So?

BARRY: Which they would have used.

SANDRA: That doesn't make it *right*.

BARRY: Only they didn't. Because, thank Christ, I managed to forestall them. (*He turns and looks at her.*) Can you please tell me why stopping that happening is *bad*?

(*But SANDRA is holding her ground, shaking her head.*)

SANDRA: I think you know it is.

BARRY: Oh, do I?

SANDRA: Of course. What you've got is an unsafe prosecution. It's crazy. If you'd been caught, you'd have lost the lot. You'd have lost everything. You still could.

BARRY: I don't know what you mean by 'if I'd been caught'. (*He looks at her a moment, then shakes his head.*) Sandra, these people are scum. We're dealing with scum. A policeman without power, that's a contradiction. They're sending us out there with *nothing* these days. They've taken all our power. So we each have to make it. You make it for yourself. And then you use it.

SANDRA: It isn't right, Barry.

(*He turns and looks at her, calmly contemptuous.*)

BARRY: Oh, really? Is that what you think?

SANDRA: Yes, it is.

(*She looks at him unforgivingly.*)

It's just stupid, it's main bloody stupid, that's the thing about you, Barry. You used to be smart. You were really smart. Until your interest got to be in beating the system. Playing your own game. Working out your grievance. And that's when you started to get really dumb. Because you lose sight of things. You're so concerned to do it your own way, to prove you're the guy who's got it over everyone else, you lose sight of what the whole point is. We're meant to make sure that the criminals go down.

BARRY: They've gone down.

SANDRA: Sure. But they went down the curly way. All you've done is lay up trouble for yourself. Because some time, at some point, someone will notice. They'll spot you, Barry. I know it. And maybe it's good that they do . . .

BARRY: Why's that?

SANDRA: Because you're a danger. You are. Your brain's somewhere else. It's not on the job. It's on the aggravation. All right, I know. For God's sake, it gets to me too. But I used to admire you.

(*He waits a moment, then starts calmly.*)

BARRY: Then, OK, that's fine. Please. Go tell the Chief Super. If it 'worries' you, then OK, go ahead. Please. Be Gary Cooper. Shit, I don't care. Better still, be Sally Field. What the world needs is another prima donna. Parade your conscience. If that's who you are. But all you'll do is make yourself despised by a lot of decent people. And that's not the clever thing it is in the films. It's long. And it's nasty. And what's worst, it's selfish, because we all know it's really about showing off. (*He turns from across the room.*) You can do that. Death or glory. Do it. You're welcome, Sandra. But no one will ever trust you again. (*He smiles.*) 'Shut up, here comes Sandra. Don't tell Sandra. Say nothing, Sandra's around.' Perhaps that's what you want. (SANDRA *doesn't answer.*)

Me, I stopped going to the movies.

(*From outside the charge room, the sudden noise of struggle, pitched loud and violent.*)

72

Let's hear it for the guys who keep turning up.

(*The charge-room door is thrown open.* TOBY *comes bursting through it, locked in the arms of a wild drunk in his fifties, really filthy and fighting mad, known as* NELSON. *They are already scrapping, so they fall together on to the desk, both shouting.*)

TOBY: Jesus Christ, get hold of him! Bloody hell, what's happening?

BARRY: Lester!

NELSON: I've had enough of this bloody bastard.

(LESTER *appears at once from the front.*)

LESTER: Now watch it, go easy, what the hell is this?

(TOBY *has struggled free of* NELSON, *who is sprawled across Lester's desk.*)

TOBY: This dickhead had just been sick on my shoes.

NELSON: You're all bloody bastards. I hate the lot of you.

(TOBY *starts to pull him off the desk, but nobody makes any attempt to help.* LESTER *simply moves round to go and sit down in his place.*)

LESTER: Oh, right, yes . . .

NELSON: I hate the bloody sodding police.

LESTER: Why can't they get a new tune? We've heard it.

(*He suddenly turns round and, from nowhere, shouts at* NELSON, *who is being messily armlocked by* TOBY.)

Do you have any idea, you stupid arsehole, how bloody boring it is for us?

(NELSON *makes a wild attempt at a punch.* TOBY *is just managing to hold it together, but* LESTER *just watches.*)

Hold him. Hold the stupid bugger. Shit, Toby, come on. Page one. Delivering a body. Please deliver a body in reasonable shape.

(TOBY *has* NELSON *straight now and under control.* BARRY *has wandered a few paces away, just watching.* SANDRA *is not moving, still where she was. And now* ESTHER *has appeared from the front, hearing the commotion.*)

TOBY: I'm sorry, Sarge.

LESTER: Your hat is crooked.

TOBY: My bollocks are crooked as well.

(LESTER *doesn't look up, just shouts.*)

LESTER: Esther!

73

ESTHER: Yeah?

LESTER: Go and rehang Toby's bollocks.

ESTHER: I know how to do that. I did the course.

(*Suddenly* BARRY *speaks, dangerous, quiet.*)

BARRY: Why not ask Sandra? She's a team player. She's a hands-on police officer. She'll always pitch in. She's always there for you.

(*He suddenly looks across the room at her. After all the noise, there is a sudden silence.*)

Aren't you? You can trust Sandra. (*He looks at her a moment, then turns and walks straight out of the room.*) Tell Jimmy I had to go home.

(*He's gone.* LESTER *does not look up from writing.* ESTHER *is anxiously looking across the room to* SANDRA.)

LESTER: Oh blimey-deary, did I miss something?

ESTHER: I think Barry's got his period.

LESTER: Yeah, that's what it is.

(NELSON *has gone to sit down on the bench, and* TOBY *is standing near him.* ESTHER *walks casually past* SANDRA.)

ESTHER: (*With a tone of real concern*) You all right, sweetheart?

(NELSON *yells before* SANDRA *can answer.*)

NELSON: You're all bloody bastards.

LESTER: Will you shut up?

(LESTER *has still not looked up.*)

SANDRA: I'm fine, I'm back on. No worries.

LESTER: Will you do a minor accident? In the Clapham Road? Esther, you go along too.

(SANDRA *goes to take the piece of paper he is holding up in his hand.* LESTER *looks up a second.*)

You all right really?

SANDRA: Sure.

(*She goes to get her jacket and put it on.* ESTHER *goes to get hers.* LESTER *writes.* NELSON *subsides.* TOBY *dreams. Sudden peace. It's the schoolroom again.* SANDRA *picks up her hat and, on the way out, speaks half to herself and half to the room.*)

No problem. I'm one of the boys.

SCENE FOUR

As SANDRA *goes we move to the shower block of the prison. In the main room, which we do not see clearly and which is suggested only by its dim outline and, most importantly, by the sound of the water jets, there are thirty or forty shower heads in the communal bathing area. At the front,* GERARD *appears, wet from the showers, with a towel wrapped round him. He is about to dry himself when another* PRISONER *appears beside him. He is older, tattooed and, although wet, still appears dirty after his shower.*

FIRST PRISONER: You see it's just this.
    (GERARD *turns.*)
GERARD: I'm sorry?
FIRST PRISONER: It's this. It's just this.
    (GERARD *looks and sees a* SECOND PRISONER *has appeared. He is younger, crew-cut and powerfully built.*)
    We need you to do something for us.
GERARD: Something for you?
FIRST PRISONER: That's right.
    (GERARD *eyes them a moment.*)
GERARD: I've got to go.
FIRST PRISONER: No. You're doing something for us.
GERARD: What's that?
    (*The two* PRISONERS *don't answer, they just stand right by him.*)
    Can I go?
FIRST PRISONER: No.
GERARD: What do you want me to do?
SECOND PRISONER: You've got to take your towel off. You've got to live life with no towel.
    (*There is a moment.* GERARD *takes one step back and looks to the opening that leads to the shower room.*)
FIRST PRISONER: Don't call for a screw. There isn't one.
SECOND PRISONER: There is one. He's not coming, though.
FIRST PRISONER: There's more of us.
    (GERARD *again looks to the gap.*)
    There's two on the door.
    (GERARD *waits a moment.*)

75

GERARD: Then what is this?

FIRST PRISONER: You've seen a black bitch.

GERARD: I'm sorry?

FIRST PRISONER: You see a black bitch, that's what they say.
(*He turns to the* SECOND PRISONER.) Turn the showers up,
will you?
(*The* SECOND PRISONER *goes out to the main room.*)
I like the noise.
(GERARD *looks as if he might try to make a run for it.*)
You know what smart people do?
(*The sound of the showers being turned up, hotter and harder.*
GERARD *doesn't answer.*)
They do their time, Gerard. They do it. They just do it. (*He
waits a moment.*) They never put themselves first.
(GERARD *is shaking now. The* FIRST PRISONER *moves closer to
him.*)
Wherever you go, we can get to you. Don't ever think there's
anywhere safe.
(*The* SECOND PRISONER *has reappeared in the opening.*)

SECOND PRISONER: Has he taken his towel off?

FIRST PRISONER: Not yet.
(*The* FIRST PRISONER *moves right up to* GERARD *and gently
reaches out to take the top of the towel around* GERARD's *waist,
as if to rip it off.*)
We want it off because we don't want blood on it.

SECOND PRISONER: You can wipe up afterwards with this.
(*The* SECOND PRISONER *has moved towards him and now
throws him a rag he has had in his hand. The* FIRST PRISONER
still has his hand on the waist of GERARD's *towel.*)

FIRST PRISONER: Is that all right?
(GERARD *cannot answer. The stage begins to darken. The*
SECOND PRISONER *walks round behind* GERARD *to put his arm
round Gerard's neck. The sound of the showers, hotter still and
louder.*)
Take him to the showers, and let's get to work.
(*As* GERARD *is seized by the* SECOND PRISONER *and pulled
backwards towards the opening, the sound of the showers drowns
out his screaming, and the lights lose them as they go.*)

Outside the chambers. At once, as GERARD *is dragged off,* IRINA
*appears, distraught, tired-looking, and, as the prison disappears, she
sees a group of men all laughing together in a clubby way, all clerks to
the lawyers, in suits, standing together.*

IRINA: Oh, Woody, there you are, I've been trying to find you.
> (*At once* WOODY *turns, sees it's* IRINA, *and detaches himself
> from the group, winking at the others, as if at some hidden joke.*)

WOODY: See you later, lads.

ALL: See you, Woody.
> (*He walks across to join* IRINA *and they head for the chambers.
> The group on the lawn disperses as they go.*)

WOODY: Yeah, I'm sorry. I've been out getting work. (*He
> indicates a bundle of briefs under his arm.*)

IRINA: It's just I needed an appointment for a word with Sir
> Peter. I've been trying for days.

WOODY: Well, you're never here.

IRINA: No.

WOODY: Running round the country. Thanks to all my efforts on
> your behalf.
> (IRINA *smiles, taking this lightly.*)
> How is it out there?

IRINA: Oh, it's great.

WOODY: Are you sure? You look shattered. Is it all getting to
> you?

IRINA: What?

WOODY: I mean the job.
> (*She stops, frowning.*)

IRINA: Did someone say that?

WOODY: No. (WOODY *looks puzzled, not understanding her
> concern.*) No, of course not. I'm joking, that's all.
> (*They go into Sir Peter's chambers in Lincolns Inn, white-
> panelled, with Georgian prints on the walls, and all the comforts
> of his profession: the fine desk, the books, the lamps.* WOODY *sets
> about sorting his papers.*)
> No, on the contrary, that's not the word on you.

IRINA: Oh, what's the word then?

WOODY: You know as well as I do. (*He grins. His tone is very light.*)
You're very popular. Sir Peter adores you.

IRINA: Yes. Yes, Woody, I know.
(WOODY *does not notice how guarded her tone is, as he arranges
the stuff on the desk.*)

WOODY: He was really excited, you should have heard him, he kept
telling me, it was what he was praying for. You were eating at
the Ritz . . .

IRINA: Yes. (*She waits, not getting the point of* WOODY's *pleasure in
this.*) So?

WOODY: Then Toppy Pilkington came in?

IRINA: That's right.
(*She frowns.* WOODY *is grinning delightedly.*)
Well?

WOODY: You see they're old rivals. Deadly!

IRINA: Rivals?

WOODY: Just in the libel court, that's all I mean.
(WOODY *smiles. She looks incomprehending.*)
He said you should have seen Toppy's expression. When he
saw Sir Peter with you, at a table for two. Toppy could barely
choke down his Lobster Thermidor.
(IRINA *frowns, interrupting.*)

IRINA: Woody, it's only appearances.

WOODY: Sure. I know that. (*He throws her a quick glance.*) No
problem.

IRINA: You do understand that? We're not involved.

WOODY: Did I say you were?
(*He still has a smile on his face as he works. Then he looks up to
find she is still looking at him.*)
Hey, lighten up. You need a sense of humour.

IRINA: Yes, I must remember. It's all a big joke.
(WOODY *looks at her a moment.*)

WOODY: It's a fine balance. You know that, Miss Platt. He's not a
fool. He wouldn't have had you as his junior unless you could
argue a case. But also . . . (*He's quieter.*) Let's face it, you've
got to play a slightly tricky game. And there's one way to do
that.

IRINA: Is there? (*She looks at him, impassive.*) How's that?

WOODY: Gracefully, Irina. (*He smiles slightly, to take the curse off it.*)

78

Do it with a smile on your face.

(*At once* SIR PETER *appears, unloading his papers.*)

And now here's Sir Peter . . .

SIR PETER: Good morning, everyone.

WOODY: I'm sorry, I should have carried your gear.

(WOODY, *like a manservant, has gone into the ritual of gathering Sir Peter's clothes and papers.* SIR PETER *smiles at* IRINA.)

SIR PETER: Irina.

IRINA: Peter. Did you have a good morning in court?

SIR PETER: Certainly. Chancery. Such a relief after criminals.
(*He turns, smiling at her.*) You know what's so boring about criminal law?

IRINA: I think I can guess.

SIR PETER: Go on.

IRINA: It involves real human beings.

(SIR PETER *smiles and gestures assent.*)

SIR PETER: That, certainly. But worse, you have to establish the facts.

(WOODY *has gone round to open a bottle of champagne.*)

That's why I also like libel cases. Because so often they're a matter of opinion. There are no facts. You're arguing about things which no one can prove. You're juggling with air, pure and simple. (*He smiles at* IRINA.) And these are the cases where I seem to do well.

WOODY: I can't think why. (*He offers* SIR PETER *a drink.*) Your glass of champagne?

SIR PETER: Yes, thank you.

(*At his desk,* SIR PETER *flicks a look at* IRINA, *sensing already she is not susceptible to his good cheer.*)

Irina?

IRINA: Not before lunch. (*Her tone stays serious, not changing.*) Our man's been beaten up.

SIR PETER: Yes, Woody mentioned.

(*He turns at once to* WOODY, *who is pouring himself a glass.*)

IRINA: He's put himself on Rule 43.

SIR PETER: Very wise.

IRINA: But I mean, I've seen him, he's in isolation, he's often banged up twenty-three hours a day. He speaks to almost no one.

79

SIR PETER: What did I tell you? Bloody criminal law!

WOODY: You said it.

SIR PETER: Touch anything criminal and there's always a mess.

> (IRINA *smiles, trying not to be put off*.)

IRINA: Yes, but in fact , as far as the case goes, the actual beating up is good news for us. It vindicates McKinnon.

SIR PETER: Do you think?

IRINA: It proves that Travis and Faulkner are frightened. They attack him because they've got something to hide.

> (SIR PETER *frowns, holding back*.)

SIR PETER: Do they?

IRINA: I'd have thought it was obvious. Surely they're police informers? Aren't they? You said that yourself.

SIR PETER: I said they could be.

IRINA: They did some sort of deal. Now plainly they're scared. Because if McKinnon comes out with it, then of course they're identified. They're in trouble with whoever they informed on. (*She smiles, as if it's QED*.) Let's face it, it's a pretty good reason for beating him up.

> (SIR PETER *smiles, sitting back*.)

SIR PETER: Irina, my dear, it was a fight in prison. Have you ever been in prison?

IRINA: Of course.

SIR PETER: I've known people fight over half an ounce of tobacco. They fight when they dislike the look of someone else's face. (*He shakes his head*.) Are you telling me – without any friendly witnesses – you can establish that this fight had one particular cause? (*He turns aside, suddenly passionate*.) And here again – here we go! – my God, do I have *déjà vu*? – *once again* in this case, it's on the word of one man. Which man? The same man.

> (IRINA *is shaking her head, disbelieving*.)

And, *once again*, there's no actual proof.

> (*He has leant forward*. IRINA *can't wait to interrupt*.)

IRINA: You don't understand. Gerard says . . .

SIR PETER: I know what Gerard *says*, but has it not occurred to you – be serious, please – Irina, this is actually the twenty-eighth day . . .

IRINA: You think I don't know?

80

SIR PETER: Today we have to lodge our grounds for appeal.
(WOODY *chips in, respectful.*)

WOODY: I was going to remind you.

SIR PETER: And you want us to argue all these convictions are
unsafe on the grounds of one unsubstantiated allegation by
one proven liar about a bag of maybe-drugs-maybe-aspirin
whose exact function not even he understands?
(IRINA *is shaking her head.*)
Whereas on the other hand – please let me finish – I can enter
a perfectly decent appeal against sentence, far easier, far
simpler, what we might call the 'lame-dog' appeal. The poor
bastard is young, he's got a wife and two children, one of
them imperfect. It's his first offence. So, on sentimental
grounds, his sentence must be cut.

IRINA: I know. (*She hesitates, uneasy now.*) I know you can do
that.

SIR PETER: If we go for a lesser sentence, we've got a good
chance.
(*He looks to her for a response.*)

IRINA: It's just . . . I can't explain. I don't want to do that.

SIR PETER: No? (*He waits a moment.*) What's your reason?

IRINA: I know this is legally meaningless. I do understand that.
(*She looks uneasily between them.*) I don't want to do it
because it isn't right.
(*At once* SIR PETER *explodes.*)

SIR PETER: Right? What's right to do with it?

IRINA: The police were on the fiddle!

SIR PETER: That's what you suspect. But it isn't our business.

IRINA: Isn't it?

SIR PETER: We've only one interest, and that's in getting our
own client out. (*He sits back, exasperated.*) I mean, just look
at it, examine it objectively, say we decided, all right,
something funny's gone on . . .

IRINA: It has.

SIR PETER: So what's the next step? We apply to the Registrar of
Appeals – always assuming he's amenable – for funds to hire
a private detective. Even if we get them – and that's a big if –
just think. This inquiry agent – some dumb Joe – he's got a
very nice job. He's got to walk up the steps of a South

London police station and go up to the six-foot hairy ape on the desk and say, 'Hold on, I wonder, could you help me? I think something fishy may have gone on round here.' (*He laughs.*)

WOODY: It doesn't sound a good way to make a living.

SIR PETER: Do you really think our man's got a chance? Of getting a confession? From an experienced detective like Barry Hopper?

IRINA: Hopper's got a sidekick.

SIR PETER: I know.

IRINA: Called Jimmy Khan. He's not impossible. I saw something there. (*She turns, improvising.*) And that policewoman, I watched her at the trial. Now, she's a human being.

(SIR PETER *is shaking his head.*)

SIR PETER: Irina, you have been my dinner-date. You simply cannot be this naïve. (*He is now up, pouring more champagne.*) It's called a force. Police *force*, that's the name for it. Everyone knows. It's the wrong word. If I could pass an Act of Parliament, I'd call it what it actually is. (*He smiles.*) 'Club.' Police club. And unless you can find someone who's interested in jacking in their membership, you haven't got a cat's chance in hell.

(IRINA *has moved across the room, not giving in.*)

IRINA: Well, that's what we must do.

SIR PETER: Oh, really! Don't be ridiculous.

IRINA: You don't believe him.

(*She has suddenly raised her voice.* SIR PETER *is taken aback.*)

SIR PETER: I'm sorry?

IRINA: You don't believe what Gerard says.

SIR PETER: That hardly matters.

IRINA: You think he's lying.

(SIR PETER *looks at her, firm now.*)

SIR PETER: He's fighting for his life. Since you ask, yes, he has a technique. Even you must have sensed it. Maximum confusion. He's under the impression that's his best chance. He lied in court. We know that. Persistently. Now those lies are all bust. So. The next stage is unfounded allegation. It's not an unfamiliar route. Discredit the police. Discredit the prison staff. Engineer an attack. Claim you're a victim. (*He stops and looks at her.*) Then find someone who'll swallow it whole.

(IRINA *is quiet now, attentive.*)

IRINA: Someone?

SIR PETER: Yes.

IRINA: Are you meaning me? Is that what you mean?

(SIR PETER *just smiles, as if no answer were needed.*)

So you think he just leads me by the nose?

SIR PETER: No. I don't think it's your nose he's got you by.

(*There is a sudden silence as if they can't quite believe what they've heard.* WOODY *shifts.*)

WOODY: I think this may be my moment to go.

IRINA: No, Woody, don't go . . .

(WOODY *hovers a moment, uncertain, between them.*)

SIR PETER: You forget I represented this man. I know him. I've represented dozens of people like him.

IRINA: *Like* him?

SIR PETER: Certainly. I do know the type.

IRINA: Oh, do you?

(IRINA *is standing now, her anger low and dangerous.*)

What type is that?

SIR PETER: You know perfectly well.

IRINA: No, I don't actually. Tell me.

SIR PETER: He's an ordinary, slightly sub-average human being who has landed himself in a damn stupid mess.

IRINA: Sub-average?

SIR PETER: Of course he's sub-average.

IRINA: How *dare* you say that?

(SIR PETER *smiles, enjoying himself.*)

SIR PETER: Think about it, Irina. It's not such a terrible thing. I hate to have to tell you, it'll come as a shock to you, but, by definition, sub-average is what nearly 50 per cent of the entire population is fated to be.

IRINA: Yes. (*She stops, a sudden lethal tone in her voice.*) No doubt. If you think in those terms.

(SIR PETER *for the first time is rattled by her.*)

SIR PETER: Look, for God's sake, it's obvious he's lying . . .

IRINA: Is it?

SIR PETER: Of course. I don't blame him. He's fighting like a rat.

IRINA: How do you *know*?

(SIR PETER *shakes his head, confident.*)

SIR PETER: After a while you do develop an instinct. That's one of the things a first-rate advocate has. Your profession, after all, is the judgement of people. After a while, you have certain skills. It's not even conscious. It becomes animal. It's a gut instinct. Here. (*He points to his heart.*) I'd say, if anything, it's *the* crucial ability. You're asked to walk every day through a minefield of lies. If nothing else, you do develop a certain forensic capacity for knowing when someone is telling the truth.

(IRINA *has moved away, quiet now, sure of herself.*)

IRINA: The other night . . .

SIR PETER: Yes?

IRINA: When we had dinner . . . you remember we had dinner at the Ritz? We were waiting for a cab. I said how much I'd enjoyed it.

(SIR PETER *smiles.*)

SIR PETER: You did.

IRINA: What a wonderful evening I'd had. (*She pauses, dangerous.*) Now, please, I'd be interested, answer me forensically, what's your opinion? (*She smiles, hanging the next question in the air.*) You say you know about these things. Was I telling the truth?

(SIR PETER *pauses, looking for the lawyer's answer.*)

SIR PETER: I would have said . . . you appeared to enjoy it.

IRINA: What did I think of *The Magic Flute*?

SIR PETER: You liked it.

IRINA: Did I?

SIR PETER: Of course. You said you did. It's a great opera. (*He hesitates a second, fatally.*) The tickets were extremely expensive.

IRINA: Oh well, in that case, it isn't in doubt.

(*She has spat out this remark so forcefully that* SIR PETER *is genuinely shocked.*)

SIR PETER: I don't know what you mean. What do you prove by this?

IRINA: I will tell you. These judgements, these 'judgements' you

84

make all the time, these judgements which seem to be graven in stone, they have only the status of prejudice.

SIR PETER: I'm sorry. That is really not true.

(IRINA *has wandered away, fired up now.*)

IRINA: Do you really not hear it? Do you never notice it? (*She characterizes:*) 'I was talking to *Woody* and he was telling me that *Toppy* was feeling green with jealousy, and *Chugger* no doubt was feeling something else . . .' (*She turns, unable to contain her bewilderment.*) And *I* am feeling . . . did I come all this way to take up residence in the pages of the *Beano*? Am I going crazy? Does no one else see? (*She looks round the room, sure of herself now.*) It seems so obvious to an outsider. Do you really not know? All this behaviour, the honours, the huge sums of money, the buildings, the absurd dressing-up. They do have a purpose. It's anaesthetic. It's to render you incapable of imagining life the other way round.

(SIR PETER *shifts, uncomfortable.*)

SIR PETER: That is simply ridiculous.

IRINA: Is it? (*She smiles.*) Is it? What about the whole joke of you, who claim this infallible instinct for deception, this forensic gift for detecting the truth? You sit there – what? – a Knight Commander of the British Empire. (*She laughs.*) You're conspiring in a lie. It's a lie. What British Empire? Hasn't word reached you? It no longer exists.

(SIR PETER *points to her, having no time to censor his reaction.*)

SIR PETER: Now, that is actually profoundly offensive.

IRINA: Is it?

SIR PETER: A knighthood is hardly a lie. It's not a lie. It's . . . a form of words.

IRINA: And there's a difference?

SIR PETER: Of course.

(*She shakes her head.*)

IRINA: It seems so clear, you see only what you want to . . .

SIR PETER: That's not true.

IRINA: 'Oh, I don't do criminal law.'

SIR PETER: I don't. (*He shifts, suspecting a trap.*) I don't like it.

IRINA: I wonder, what's the reason for that?

SIR PETER: I've said. Intellectually.

IRINA: I'll tell you the reason. When you take on a civil case, it's a clear forty thousand just for taking the brief.

(SIR PETER *turns at once to* WOODY.)

SIR PETER: Have you been disclosing my figures?

WOODY: No.

IRINA: Plus your refreshers. Fifteen hundred a day. (*She laughs, enjoying herself.*) The intellectual attractions of civil law become suddenly apparent.

(SIR PETER *is at once vehement.*)

SIR PETER: It makes absolutely no difference. I bring the same skills and attitudes, whatever I'm paid.

IRINA: Do you? (*She looks at him.*) Do you really? Woody said, before I insisted, you had decided in McKinnon's case not even to appeal. On *any* grounds.

(SIR PETER *swings round on* WOODY *at once.*)

SIR PETER: Did you tell her that?

WOODY: Well, no, I . . .

IRINA: Hold on, Woody.

SIR PETER: No, let's get this clear.

(WOODY *pauses, hating this situation.*)

WOODY: I hinted at it. I thought that was fair.

SIR PETER: Woody, I'm shocked at you.

IRINA: Please, the issue is not Woody's loyalty. That's the oldest trick of them all. Address the leak and take no notice of the issue. (*She waits a moment.*) Is it true you were going to let the whole verdict stand?

(SIR PETER *is calm now.*)

SIR PETER: Yes. Yes, since you ask me. (*He stops, unapologetic.*) The case was not interesting.

IRINA: Not interesting to *you.*

SIR PETER: It had no distinguishing features. There was no pressure from his solicitor . . .

IRINA: Well, no, there wouldn't be.

SIR PETER: And I was satisfied I'd done what I could.

(*She looks at him as he looks up at her, level, serious.*)

IRINA: I attended the trial, remember?

SIR PETER: So?

IRINA: I watched you at work. You stumbled over their names. You even called your own client 'McPherson' at one point.

SIR PETER: Irina, I was given the brief overnight. That happens.

Three-quarters of all criminal briefs are returned the night
before a trial. Because a barrister becomes unavailable.

IRINA: And the law, of course, must be run at the court's
convenience.

(SIR PETER *suddenly flares at this*.)

SIR PETER: So what are you saying? Did I let him down?

IRINA: You'd have just let him *rot*.

(SIR PETER *nods, defiant*.)

SIR PETER: Of course. Because I'm not a crusader. It's not in the
brief. Nor should it be. We shouldn't be . . . soggily
compassionate about every petty larcenist we're hired to
represent. Indeed it's actually dangerous. Because the fact is
. . . your judgement then goes. As yours is going, Irina. (*He
looks at her, beady now*.) There is a glass screen. And our
clients, I'm afraid, live on one side of it. We on the other.
And, much as you may wish it, we cannot break through.

(IRINA *turns and smiles at* WOODY, *who is just watching at the
side*.)

IRINA: Woody, this appeal we're discussing, which seems to us so
urgent, tell us, when will it be heard?

WOODY: Twelve months.

IRINA: Yes.

WOODY: Maybe ten if we're lucky.

IRINA: Yes. When the judges are ready. What state will Gerard
be in by then?

(SIR PETER *watches, not answering now*.)

Oh yes, every one of us, we all feel self-righteous, we all say
what *we* do is fine . . . (*She stops*.) And meanwhile we're
losing him. I go in there. I'm watching him vanish. (*She
looks at* SIR PETER.) And each person says, 'Oh, you mustn't
blame me . . .'

(*The room is silent now, as if some bridge were crossed, as if* SIR
PETER *at last hears her*.)

But it isn't quite true. Well, is it? You've just told me. You
could have done more. Couldn't you? (*She waits*.) Couldn't
you?

(SIR PETER *nods slightly*.)

SIR PETER: Yes. And I now shall.

(*She smiles at the lawyer's answer*.)

87

I've taken you in. I've given you a tenancy. There are
thousands of young counsel who'd kill for the chance. (*He
looks at her, a little tenderness apparent.*) I've always been
kind.

IRINA: Yes. I know that. Your gift is for making me aware of
that. (*She smiles.*) I am conscious . . . it's in your power to be
kind. At every meal. Throughout every opera. In the
morning, when I come in. At your wish. By your permission.
(*She looks at him.*) It's hard to say thank you ten times a day.
Because the effort is finally demeaning. I hardly remember,
but I was five when my father died. (*She thinks a moment.*) So
I've got on without one. I don't need another. Not now. No,
thank you.

(*She gets up and starts to walk out of the room. She is quite calm.
She smiles at* WOODY *as she goes out.*)

I hope that was graceful enough.

SCENE SIX

Crystal Palace. IRINA *is standing at the top of the hill, right by the
great radio mast. She is slightly hidden. Below her, London is laid
out, glimmering at dusk on a summer evening. The wind is blowing
gently, the air is light. Then* SANDRA *appears in blue jeans and a
blouson, walking through the park.* IRINA *steps out where* SANDRA
can see her. SANDRA *stops.*

IRINA: No, it's not chance.

(SANDRA *looks at her a moment.*)

SANDRA: What is this?

(IRINA *doesn't answer.*)

I know who you are. I saw you . . .

IRINA: Yes.

SANDRA: At that trial. I don't have to talk to you.

IRINA: No.

SANDRA: It's against the rules.

IRINA: Well, loosely. Technically, yes.

(IRINA *waits to see if* SANDRA *will go on.*)

SANDRA: You know I can shop you.

88

IRINA: Sure. I'm aware of that.

SANDRA: Improper approaches.

IRINA: I've not said a thing.

SANDRA: Not yet.

IRINA: I don't think you'd shop me.

SANDRA: Wouldn't I?

IRINA: No.

SANDRA: Why not? You've chosen a woman. Does that make you
feel safer? Why didn't you choose Jimmy? Or Barry? You
thought I'd be easier. I sort of resent that.
(For the first time they both smile.)

IRINA: You're free. You don't have to stay.
*(SANDRA looks at her a moment, then makes a little move, just a
few paces away, to look out over London. IRINA waits.)*
So. Is this where you live?

SANDRA: Nearby. Selhurst Park. When I was a kid we walked
over this hill every week. To watch Crystal Palace.

IRINA: Is that the sports team?

SANDRA: Yes. They play football.

IRINA: Ah, yes. I've done my best to understand England, but
some of the nuances pass me right by.
(SANDRA smiles at this.)

SANDRA: Crystal Palace don't have many nuances.
(But IRINA is not fazed; she just goes on talking gently.)

IRINA: Is football an interest of yours?

SANDRA: It was my Dad. He used to take me. He'd walk me over
the hill to eat fish and chips. I'd stand outside the pub while
he had a couple of lagers. *(She smiles.)* He was trying to bring
me up as a boy.

IRINA: Oh dear . . .

SANDRA: No, it was nice . . . at least when I discovered. I'd kind
of taken it for granted I was male. But that made it specially
interesting, you know, when I was fourteen or fifteen. And I
found out that I was a girl.

IRINA: Was your Dad a copper?

SANDRA: Yes.

IRINA: I guessed.

SANDRA: Is it really that obvious?
(They both laugh.)

He was great. He had this brilliant idea. That policing was really exciting. He said you're out on your own. Your own boss. It's you and the public. There's no one to tell you you're getting it wrong. You learn on the job. You learn by doing it. Each time you go out, you start over. It's you and them.

(*She stops and thinks a moment.*)

He complained. But he never stopped loving it.

IRINA: And is that how you feel?

SANDRA: Oh, yeah, it's great. It's great while you're doing it. But it's sometimes hard to come home.

(*She gives her a slightly nervous glance, her real feelings on show, and* IRINA *picks up on her tone.*)

IRINA: You know why I'm here?

SANDRA: Probably.

IRINA: It's this terrible frustration of knowing something . . . something tricky has happened and then not being able to find any proof.

(SANDRA *looks at her impassively, not giving anything away.*)

You see, I know . . . I know there was some sort of fiddle . . .

SANDRA: Go on.

IRINA: I know what occurred.

SANDRA: You don't *know*.

IRINA: No. I can guess.

(SANDRA *still doesn't react.*)

But until I can find that one individual . . . I need an individual . . . I need a friend inside the police.

SANDRA: Yes. I can see.

(SANDRA *looks at her a moment, then moves away slightly.*)

IRINA: My client got beaten up.

SANDRA: Yes. I heard that.

(*There's a pause,* IRINA *confident that she has Sandra's interest.*)

Why did that happen?

IRINA: To shut him up.

SANDRA: Are you sure? Any witnesses?

(IRINA *shakes her head.*)

Well, then you haven't a case.

IRINA: No.

(SANDRA *shrugs slightly, but* IRINA *knows she is still hooked.*)

I'm in trouble at work because of this. They say it's a quite unexceptional case. Which it is. To me that's the point. (*She is suddenly quiet*.) But they have a way of making you feel you're a bore and an idiot for wanting the truth of something. Do you know that feeling?

SANDRA: No. Never had it.

IRINA: You see, when you're training, it's the great cliché. A lawyer should never be emotionally involved. Not a day goes by when they don't mention this. 'Only a bad advocate gets too close to his case.' They love it, they say it over and over. It's like they can't say it enough. They say it a thousand times. They say it so often you turn round and think . . . now what exactly are you trying to hide?

(SANDRA *frowns*.)

SANDRA: But it's true.

IRINA: Is it?

SANDRA: Sure.

IRINA: To me it's the alibi. It's the great alibi.

SANDRA: It's being a professional.

IRINA: Is that what it is? (*She smiles*.)

SANDRA: It's like in the police. I know, I've been through this. You let a lot by. You have to.

IRINA: Do you?

SANDRA: Yeah. Yeah. Certainly. Or else you'd go crazy.

(SANDRA *looks at her, unapologetic*. IRINA *is quiet again*.)

IRINA: So how do you choose when it's time to say no?

(SANDRA *looks at her for a moment now*. IRINA *makes a slight move towards her with a card*.)

I've written my number here. In case you want to call me.

SANDRA: Thank you.

IRINA: In case you decided . . . you might change your mind.

(SANDRA *takes the card, not moving yet*.)

I was going to walk out. Yes. At one point. This was just a week or two ago. I thought, I can't take it here. Then I thought, if I go, just how exactly will that help my client? And the answer is, not at all. (*She smiles*.) I don't know, I was thinking I should move to radical chambers. There's something they call the alternative bar. Perhaps it would suit me better.

91

(*She looks and sees* SANDRA *has a smile on her face.*)

Why are you smiling? What are you smiling at?

(SANDRA *just shakes her head, a real warmth suddenly between the two women.*)

Please tell me.

SANDRA: Because there's nothing called the alternative police.

IRINA: No . . .

(*They both smile together, joined by the thought.*)

No, I know that . . .

SANDRA: There isn't a kind of nice lot who all read the *Guardian* and eat salad for lunch . . .

(IRINA *smiles.*)

You can't join another lot. Not in my profession. You see, in my line of work there's only one crowd.

(*The two women smile, a little diffidently. Then they head off separately, small against the vastness of the evening.*)

IRINA: Goodbye, Sandra. Good luck.

SCENE SEVEN

As SANDRA *goes, the court assembles. The High Court. There are fewer people than for the original trial – counsel on either side, ushers, the clerks, and, above the scene, on a raised platform, places for the three presiding judges. Light is thrown down from the high, opaque ceiling in a vivid square. At once, as the court assembles, the* USHER *stands to make her announcement.*

USHER: Silence. All rise.

(*Through a small door at the back come three High Court judges, in black, with* CUDDEFORD *in the centre. Before he takes the seat in the middle he bows to the court and then to the counsel, who bow back. The judges sit.*)

CLERK: The case of the Crown versus McKinnon in the Court of Appeal, set down to be heard at two o'clock, Mr Justice Cuddeford presiding.

(CUDDEFORD *nods to the counsel.*)

CUDDEFORD: Counsel.

SIR PETER: My Lords. (*He stands.*)

May it please your Lordships, Miss Platt will shortly be
joining me to appear for the appellant. My learned friend Mr
Bird represents the Crown.

(CUDDEFORD *acknowledges them.*)

CUDDEFORD: We have read the papers in the case. We will listen to
any further submissions, or any witnesses counsel may wish to
call.

SIR PETER: My Lords, I have no witnesses. As you will
understand, it is not part of our case that the evidence itself
should in any way be reviewed. The case was conducted with
impeccable fairness by the original trial judge, we have no
complaints as to the merit of the verdict. Furthermore, we do
not question or fault in any way the behaviour of the police.

(*As he says this the light begins to fade in the courtroom, and* BARRY
*is seen to get up and leave the court through the door into the corridor
outside. He lights a cigarette as* SIR PETER *is heard to go on.*)

The plea we are making is purely and simply a plea for
clemency. We are putting ourselves at the court's mercy,
asking you to consider the exceptional pressures of
circumstance which caused my client to embark on what I can
assure you now will be a short-lived career in crime.

(*Along the corridor, hurrying, comes* IRINA *in wig and gown. Just
before she reaches the court's door, she drops a paper, but does not
notice.* BARRY *smoking his cigarette, nods at it.*)

BARRY: You dropped a paper.

IRINA: Thank you.

(*He stands and watches her stoop for it.*)

BARRY: Aren't you a bit late?

IRINA: I had another case. There was a jam on the M40.

BARRY: Working you, are they?

IRINA: And what are you doing here?

(*She has stood up now and is facing him. He carries on smoking.*)

BARRY: Oh. Another case, too. I was just dropping by.

IRINA: What, to make sure there's no danger?

(*He looks at her mistrustfully.*)

No challenge to the evidence?

BARRY: I didn't see any sign of the boy.

IRINA: No. He doesn't attend. It's his appeal but he doesn't
attend it.

BARRY: Yeah. (*He smiles, nonchalant.*) It's a funny old world.

(*He is about to walk away, but* IRINA *can't resist going on.*)

IRINA: I heard you got a medal.

BARRY: That's right.

IRINA: I know how you got it.

(BARRY *looks at her. Her gaze does not waver.*)

If it's of interest, I know what you did.

(*He looks at her a moment, giving nothing away.*)

BARRY: Do you?

IRINA: I know you think – you think it doesn't matter.

BARRY: Do you?

IRINA: You cut a few corners and you think, what's the harm?

BARRY: Is that what you think? (*He smiles.*) God, you must really understand us.

IRINA: It isn't hard, is it?

BARRY: Isn't it?

IRINA: I do understand how policemen's minds work.

BARRY: Do you? From what? From your experience? From your deep experience of doing a filthy, thankless job? You really know? Oh, do you? (*He leans in towards her.*) When was anyone last sick on your wig?

(IRINA *almost loses her temper, suddenly taken away by anger, impulsively reaching out for his arm as he moves away.*)

IRINA: Oh, come on, that's a shitty argument . . .

(BARRY *swings round, suddenly dangerous, after being touched on the arm.*)

BARRY: You really want to scrap with me? Do you?

(IRINA *stands shocked by his sudden violence.*)

You really want to fight? Do you? Please? Outside. No problem. What is it? Queensberry Rules?

IRINA: What's the point? I'm sure you'd pretty soon find a way round them.

BARRY: Oh, that's very smart.

(*Now* IRINA *turns, under control again, and starts to move away to the courtroom, but as she does so, he calls out to her.*)

What do you want? What do you people want? Except to tell other people how to do their jobs? Listen, why don't you go and sit on a committee? Yeah, isn't that the English way? A lot of middle-class people sit on a committee and then they

94

tell us what we're all doing wrong? (*He smiles contentedly.*)
Yeah. That's it. That's what we'd like. Please. We'd value it.
Sure. I think it's one thing the police really need. More
advice. That's it, we love it. We can't get enough. Especially
from people who don't do the job.
(IRINA *shakes her head, then moves back across the space to take
him on.*)

IRINA: You don't bullshit me. I see right through it. All this
bullshit drill-sergeant stuff. It's feeble. (*She suddenly moves
towards him.*) You broke the rules. You did. The police have
got to do better than that.
(BARRY *smiles.*)

BARRY: You may be right. It's not important. It doesn't matter,
you see. Call me stubborn, or what. But I tell you what, I tell
you. I don't take lectures on ethics from lawyers.
(*He looks up at her, closer now.*)
Put your hand on your heart, could you say I was wrong?
(*He breaks into a broad smile.* WOODY *comes out of the court and
is standing silently behind* IRINA.)

WOODY: Cuddeford's about to deliver. Miss Platt, you'd better
come in.
(BARRY *steps back.*)

BARRY: I've got to be going. I'd love to have a drink with you one
day. Call me up if you like. (*He smiles.*) It's not hard to find
me. My name's in the book.
(IRINA *turns and goes back into the court. As she does so, the
lights change to emphasize the court. We hear* CUDDEFORD
picked up in mid-speech.)

CUDDEFORD: Sir Peter presents the case of his client with an
eloquence which is hard to fault. We are satisfied the
prisoner's inexperience, his youth, his gullibility, the tragic
circumstances of his young family, all these should weigh
heavily, and were not, in our opinion, taken sufficiently into
account. For these reasons, we are pleased to say, we have no
hesitation in reducing the prisoner's sentence from five years
to four and a half.
(*The moment he says this, the stage darkens at once, and, before
any response comes, the court disperses.*)

The court disperses, and the stage expands again to the shape it was for
Act I Scene Six, in which IRINA *first visited the prison. But it is*
gloomier than ever, dark, strangely quiet, and absolutely deserted
except for a bunch of officers standing together on a landing, like
sheriffs before a gunfight. IRINA *walks alongside* BECKETT, *the same*
journey she made with him on that first day.

IRINA: It's quiet.
BECKETT: Yes.
IRINA: It's really eerie.
BECKETT: There's a drug search. They're all in their cells.
IRINA: I see.
BECKETT: Each cell's being searched. So no one's allowed out.
　　They're all locked up. No exercise, no association.
IRINA: How long's it taking?
BECKETT: Oh, only a day.
　　(*In the distance, as they come on to the landing, some men yell*
　　one to another from behind the bars.)
IRINA: Still, I heard on the radio you're getting a new prison
　　inquiry. To improve conditions. You must be pleased.
BECKETT: Miss Platt, the only countries that have decent prisons
　　are the ones where the government themselves have just been
　　let out.
IRINA: Yes.
　　(*They come to Gerard's cell. The door is closed.* IRINA *slows as*
　　she reaches it.)
　　How is he feeling? Has anyone told him? Does he know the
　　verdict?
BECKETT: To be honest, he hasn't asked.
IRINA: Hasn't he?
BECKETT: No.
IRINA: Is that unusual?
　　(BECKETT *pauses a second before opening the door.*)
BECKETT: You can decide for yourself.
　　(*The door is opened.* GERARD *is standing with his back to us,*
　　completely still, looking up to the window. BECKETT *goes.*
　　IRINA *waits. It is silent.*)

IRINA: Gerard.
(He doesn't turn.)
Gerard.
(And he turns. She is still outside the tiny cell. He stays in. He stares at her.)
GERARD: You've come to see me.
IRINA: Yes.
GERARD: What do you want?
(IRINA frowns.)
IRINA: It's your appeal.
GERARD: Ah, sure. *(He flicks a glance at her, still not moving.)* Did it happen?
IRINA: Yes. They took off six months.
(He shows no reaction at all. IRINA shifts, uncomfortable.)
The whole thing was absolutely outrageous. We thought . . . we thought we could get you much less. Somehow we thought we'd do better.
GERARD: I'm sure.
IRINA: It's four and a half. That's what they're giving you.
GERARD: All right. *(He waits again.)* Thank you, then. Thanks very much.
(IRINA stands a moment, a little lost.)
Barbara's gone. Did you know that?
IRINA: No.
GERARD: Yeah. With the kiddies. To her mother's in Belfast. She couldn't carry on here. Not enough money coming into the house . . .
IRINA: No, well, that happens.
GERARD: On her own in London, no way she could survive.
(IRINA nods.)
IRINA: So she can't visit you? Unless they move you?
GERARD: That's not what they do. They don't do that. They decide everything. *(He holds up the book he has in his hand.)* Still, thank God for literature, eh?
(IRINA looks down.)
IRINA: I'm sorry, Gerard. I'm feeling awful.
GERARD: Forget it.
(She smiles.)
IRINA: Do you remember? I said I'd be your friend. And I will.

I'll keep coming. It's something I want. Not to say, 'Oh, we're all in separate compartments . . .'

GERARD: But we are. Aren't we?

(*He just looks at her.*)

IRINA: I'm hoping not.

(*He watches as she makes a slight move away.*)

Can I bring you some books?

GERARD: I've got books. (*He smiles.*) It's a book on Irish history. I've never been interested. But I'm sort of interested now. (*He moves to the floor of the cell.*) When I was brought up, it was always a background. But I laughed it off. It's funny. I wonder why I did that. What I'm saying is . . . I'm not laughing now.

(*He nods.* IRINA *looks down. She takes his hand.*)

IRINA: No.

GERARD: Goodbye, Irina.

IRINA: Goodbye.

(*She has taken a few steps away and* GERARD *is standing now, lounging against the doorjamb. She turns back slightly as he speaks again.*)

GERARD: It's like the world's saying we've got a part for you. It's like everyone's saying, there's a part you can play. All right, then, I'll play it. (*He smiles.*) I'll take this role.

(*There is a moment's silence, then very quietly, under the scene, the overture of* The Magic Flute *begins to play again.* IRINA *goes. On another part of the stage light comes up on* SANDRA, *who is sitting, facing front, thinking. At first it is dark but for the two of them. Then out of the darkness we hear* LESTER *and* ESTHER *talking behind* SANDRA.)

LESTER: Have you read this? There's a bloke here, he's accused of having sex with a dolphin. Have you read this, Esther – it's in the paper?

ESTHER: No, I haven't seen it.

LESTER: He was found by two underwater policemen. No, I'm not kidding you, that's what it says.

(*Now as the music begins to build, so do the lights, so we see* LESTER *at his desk, reading to* ESTHER, *while, in another part of the stage,* SIR PETER *is greeting* WOODY.)

SIR PETER: Good morning, Woody.

WOODY: Good morning, Sir Peter. I thought you might be looking pretty pleased.

SIR PETER: Oh, you heard?

WOODY: Yesterday. In the Chancery Division. You got one over Toppy.

SIR PETER: I did. I flattened him. Pow! On the mat.

WOODY: That's marvellous.

SIR PETER: His legs went under him. And let me tell you, he wasn't getting up for the bell.

WOODY: That's great, because, also, I tell you, we were having some fun around here . . .

(*Now, the music still builds, the prison area comes to life, with warders and prisoners starting the morning ritual of slopping out.*)

BECKETT: Slopping out! Slopping out everyone! Get ready lads, slopping out when you're ready!

(*In another part of the stage* BARRY *appears, talking to some unseen colleagues.*)

BARRY: Good morning, all. I don't think I got the grasp of this Flying Squad. I been up all night. It's way out of order. I mean, I'm trying to understand it, but your expenses system, it's a bureaucratic world of it's own.

(IRINA *stands up nervously in a fifth area and addresses an unseen meeting.*)

IRINA: Good evening, everyone, and welcome to the first meeting of the John Wilkes Society, which, as most of you know, will be a forum for lawyers concerned about the state of our modern penal system. I'm only sorry there are so few of us here. (*She pauses a second.*) It's in the nature of our job . . .

(JIMMY *breezes into the charge room.*)

LESTER: Hey, Jimmy, good morning.

JIMMY: Morning, all.

LESTER: There's an educational item I'm reading here. It concerns some of our watery brethren . . .

(ESTHER *is reading the paper over Lester's shoulder.*)

ESTHER: I'd rather have a dolphin than most of the men that I know.

(*And now the different areas all come to life, dovetailing the different things they have to say, while the music builds around them.*)

WOODY: Those new clients, you know, they just had a panic.

IRINA: Our president even is on a case in Singapore . . .

BARRY: You see I got the H4, like you told me . . .

IRINA: And can't be here tonight . . .

WOODY: Just before they were due to start their bottle went.

IRINA: And I also have a list of well-wishers . . .

LESTER: There were two coppers in wet suits, I promise you . . .

SIR PETER: That's marvellous . . .

BARRY: The H4, you know, like in the regular police, it's fine, it
    gets you into golden time, no problem . . .

IRINA: Who are right behind us . . .

LESTER: I promise you, I'm not kidding . . .

WOODY: They wanted to stop the litigation, but it was too late.

IRINA: But who can't get to our actual meeting tonight . . .

LESTER: They were positioned under the sea. Here, let me read
    you this.
    (*He laughs and adjusts the paper to read from it.* IRINA *gets out a
    piece of paper to read from that.* BARRY *gets out his expenses
    claim.* WOODY *starts gesturing with the brief. In the prison
    slopping out begins, a chain of prisoners moving across the area
    with their buckets. And now all areas start talking at once.*)
    'Police in the Lake District last night were refusing to release
    any further details in the case of an unemployed male,
    believed to be in his thirties, who has been arrested by
    members of the local force on a charge of interfering with
    two dolphins. It is understood that the man, whose identity
    was not disclosed, had been under surveillance for some
    time, and was finally arrested by two policemen who had
    stationed themselves with suitable breathing equipment at a
    place where they could observe the underwater crime. Chief
    Superintendent Hardy commended the ingenuity and
    perseverance of his men. He said that this was probably a
    one-off operation and he did not foresee that there would be
    any likely need for any further investigations of the same
    nature.' Well, no.
    (*Simultaneously with:*)

WOODY: Yeah, they'd delivered the brief. A bloke came running
    round, he said, 'Have you actually got it?' I held it up, I said,
    'It's in my hand.' He said, 'Oh God, don't tell me . . . That's
    forty thousand plus fifteen hundred a day.' I said, 'Yes, plus

secretarial, this sort of case, don't forget, I don't have to tell you, you'll find the duplicator's running all night.' He looked at me, he said, 'Have you actually got it? In that very envelope?' He said, 'Where do you live? Have you got a garage? Do you need a new loft? What do you drive? Have you got a Jaguar?' What could I say? 'I've got a Jaguar. And I like to see Sir Peter do well?' I said, 'What can I say? You know, you delivered the brief, I hate to have to tell you it's the custom we have. Once it's in hand, sorry, mate, more than my life's worth, once you put it in hand, you have to come through. Also, you know, there's another thing, I mean look at it my way . . .'
(*Simultaneously with*:)

BARRY: But here it's like they're saying, oh no, you know it's no good. You think, oh, if they spent half the time trying to support the actual coppers, I mean, getting behind us and helping to get on with the job, if they spent half the time they do thinking up ways of not paying us, then, God knows, we'd all be much better off. Because, I tell you, there isn't a system devised, not one, not one that is conceived in the human brain that any self-respecting copper isn't going to see as a challenge and think, OK, right now, how do I get round it this time? Now look, I mean, for instance, this clothing allowance, I looked this up, look, the question of professional clothing, what you have to wear on undercover work, I mean, I can't walk into a place in my new Armani, or else my cover's blown before I even start.
(*Simultaneously with*:)

IRINA: First of these is Toby Ellington, who you will all know, who's sent a message saying, yes, this is exactly the kind of action that's needed in the legal profession, how pleased he is, and how, you know, if it were any other day, but he's of course defending in the Irish case; he's of course defending in the Irish case; card here also from Lord Bethredge, who's thrilled at the idea. Also, I'm pleased to say we've had some cheques, which is excellent, from Larry Solto, of course, Jim Hail. Mary Handsworth. Basil Hart. All saying, yes, this is exactly the pressure we need to try and make sure the public understand that the legal profession at large is infinitely more sensitive and responsive than perhaps some of the more prominent dinosaurs make us appear. We do care. We are interested. We do want to see reform, and we're by no means satisfied with the lawyer's traditional image of someone who is only concerned with the administration of the law, and not with the direction it takes. Messages also from Freddy Parker . . . Bill Sopwith . . . a very nice letter here from Jane Smart . . .

(*All through this, the prisoners are slopping out in the middle of it, and before the music drowns them all out,* SANDRA *stands up. At once the music stops. She straightens her uniform, turns and takes a few paces to the centre of the stage.*)

SANDRA: I want the Chief Superintendant. (*She waits.*) I wonder. Could I have a word?

(*Darkness.*)